YOUNG WRITERS

WRITE AND SHINE!

LANCASHIRE

First published in Great Britain in 1995 by
POETRY NOW
1-2 Wainman Road, Woodston,
Peterborough, PE2 7BU

HB ISBN 1 85731 989 3
SB ISBN 1 85731 994 X

Foreword

Cock-a-doodle-doo, wakey wakey, write and shine!

Welcome to this selection of poems by young writers from your area. The poems you are about to read express thoughts and feelings on a wide range of themes which are close to the poets' hearts. All the poems in this anthology vary in style, content and subject and we hope that you enjoy reading them as much as we did editing them.

So why don't you start your day with a generous serving of poems drenched in imagination and topped with a sprinkling of emotion.

Sarah Andrew
Editor

CONTENTS

Albany High School

Paul O'Sullivan	1
Helen Fairhurst	2
Catherine Houghton	2
Elizabeth Draper	3
Victoria Danify	4

Balderstone Community High School

Gerard Tod	4
Humanyun Ashraf	5
Ghulam Hussain	6
Vicki Ward	6
Shabnam Kauser	7
Mohd Zubair Bhutta	7
Wayne Shailer	8
Khalesa Nessa	8
Amina Begum	9
Zaira Bi	9
Jodie Atkins	10
Philip Deane	10
Tejal Chauhan	11
Andrew Mallon	11
Hamara Ahmed	12
Becky Schofield	13
John Holt	13
Nausheen Bibi	14
Deborah Taylor	15
Paul Taylor	15
Katherine Robinson	16
Vicki Louise McKenzie-Lunn	16
Ian Sharp	17
Tahira Mukhtar	17
Umar Saeed	18
Emma Cottam	18
Sarah Ward	19
Qumar Mahmud	19
Naveed Haaris Sahraouei	20

Basharat Hussain	20
Doliz Miah	21
Nadeem Tariq	21
Jody Margerison	22
Monwara Begum	22
Tahira Akhtar	23
Mannié A	23
Nighat Kauser	24
Joanne Burgess	24
Naz K	25
Shaista Kauser	26
Emma Williams	27
Gemma Lee	28
Israr Hussain	28
Shabana Anwar	29
Susan Garvey	30
Zia Uddin	30
Julie Jones	31
Emma Patterson	32
Claire Cocker	33
Chanine Harris	34
Suzanne Cliffe	35
Karen Whittles	36
Kelly Gray	37
Nadia Sultana	37
Jaclyn Bell	38
Ambar Rashid	39
Carly Welsh	40
Cheryl Anne McKenna	40
Catherine McManus	41
Stephen Russell	41
Gillian Hinds	42
Nicola Hall	43
Mike Stapleton	44
Cheryl Hill	45
Ashyia Rafique	46
Maria Beadsworth	47
Muhammad Irfan	48

	Andrew Blackshaw	49
Beardwood School		
	Lisa Critchley	50
	Mary Davidson	50
	Mandee Corkin	51
	Tubassum Asghar	51
	Shabana Hussain	52
Beaumont College		
	Avril Hardman	52
Carr Hill High School		
	Michelle Lund	53
	Donna Bates	53
	Matthew Baker	54
	Sarah Wright	55
	Cassandra Goodes	56
	Sophie Cunningham	57
Crompton House School		
	Zoë Bell	58
Darwen Moorland High School		
	Naila Nisar	59
	Laura Farran	59
	Elizabeth Taylor	60
	Alex Hannon	61
	Kirsty Ure	61
	Mathew Banks	62
	Nicola Dinsdale	62
	Westley Pickup	63
	Claire Dean	64
	Julia Tomlinson	65
	Joanne Louise Burrow	66
	Bernadette O'Brien	67
	Leanne Youd	68
Fulwood High School		
	Peter Monks	68
	Paul Anderton	69
	Pinky Kaur	69
	Chris Stevenson	70
	Jamie Roskell	71

Natalie Rees	71
Andrew Ashworth	72
Emma Worrell	72
Julie Oldfield	73
Hitesh Tailor	74
Darren Jackson	75
Vicky Pickles	76
Beth Squire	77
Daniel Huntley	78

Garstang High School

Erica Fowler	79
Andrew Crook	80
Karen Cross	81
Rachel Goldspink	82
Laura Newton	83
David Parker	84
Victoria Speedwell	85
Alex Sharp	86

Gawthorpe High School

Nicola Guyer	87
Rebecca Greenwood	88

Haslingden High School

Farzana Gul	89
John Breeze	89

Hathershaw School

Lucy Deaville	90

Highfield High School

Carly Urquhart	91

Kersal High School

Lukvinder Kaur	92
Claire Hyde	93
Daniel Norris	94
Rachael Hunter	95
David W Jones	96
Emma Wilkinson	97
Sarah Liza Barrow	98
James Creely	99

Lancaster Royal Grammar School

David M Cole	100

Lytham St Anne's High School

Helen Audsley	101
Hanan Souaidi	102
Jeff Gaskell & Christian Elliott	103
Helen Smith	104
James Palmer	105
Adam Mercer	106
Kathryn Moore	107
Laura Mallinson	107
Natalie Wood	108
Hilary Stuart	108
Kate Rogan	109
Vicky Haslingden & Amy McDonald	110
Victoria Hornby	111
Tom Wigham	112

Montgomery High School

Tim Cox	113
Philip Blackwell	114

Our Lady's High School, Preston

Kimberly Hall	114
Noel Billington	115
Catherine Hughes	115
Lisa Gornall	116
Caroline Quinn	116
Lynsey Turner	117
Justine Machin	117
Jenny Clegg	118
Joanne Haggis	118
Kate Loughran	119
Christopher T Bowker	119
Shelley Hull	120
Emma Williams	120
Elizabeth Anne Smith	121
Gregory Winders	121

Jennifer L Gardner 122
Amy Wright 122
Laura Wilkinson 123
Lucia Cornacchione 123
Donna Louise Marie Massey 124
Jane L Eydmann 124
Andrew Hunter 125
Joseph O'Malley 125
Amanda Jackson 126
Michael Ainsworth 126
Dawn Austin 127
Zoë Chadwick 127
Natalie Dignan 128
Rachel Kelly 129
Katharine Lonsdale 130
Thomas Nolan 131
Wendy Nugent 132
Helen McDonnell 132
Lisa McGinty 133
Lee Steel 133
Vicky Whittle 134
Mark Foster 135
Mark Cronin 136
Katharine Reid 137
Joanne McHugh 137

Our Lady's High School, Lancaster
Claire Bottomley 138
Charlotte Youren 138
Sarah Kingston 139
Michelle Williams 140
Kerry O'Hare 141
Michael Lewis 142
Liam Dawson 143
Philip McGlone 144

Our Lady and St John RC High School
Alex Turner 145
Amanda Holden 145
Stephen Johnston 146

Daniel Hodgson	146
Emma Greaves	147
Debbie Inward	147
Emma Brown	148
Matthew Baldwin	149

Park High School

James Whalley	149
Abigail Driver	150
Rachel Hardman	151
Janine Thompson	152
Peter Odor	152
Sarah Foster	153
Jodi Carlisle	154
Gina Sarfas	154
Sarah Hesketh	155
Laura Wightman	156
John McCaul	156
Beth Turley	157
Tracy Wilkinson	157
Catherine Hall	158
Deborah Stansfield	158

Parklands High School

Darren Kirkham	159
Carla Hayes	160
Sarah Masheter	160
Gemma Hodkinson	161
Geraldine Morey	162
Iain Jackson	163

Priory High School, Penwortham

Jennifer Worthington	163
Paul Duckworth	164
Ruth Halstead	164
Matthew Procter	165
Gillian Foster	166
Richard Henfield	167
Elaine Butler	168
Sarah Preisner	168
Lisa Clements	169

Matthew Burton	169
Anita Vaza	170

Priory High School, Burscough

Sarah Durant	171
Andrew Crosbie	171
Ruth Belshaw	172
Katie Diane Halsall	173
Peter Langley	173
Ricktha Miah	174
Claire Hale	174
Ian Williams	175
Paul Blythin	175
Gemma Cox	176
Lynne Butterworth	176
Cheryl Pallett	177
Jennie Comber	177
Matthew Wright	178
Amy Dunn	178
Sally Smith	179
Sarah Holman	180
Joanne Partridge	181
Suzanne Cocks	182
James Norris	183

Rhyddings High School

Jane Ashley	183
Louise Paintin	184
Ross Mackey	185
Joanne Mainon	186
Ruth Williams	187
Emma Grundy	188

Ribblesdale High School

Tom Jeffs	188
Nicola Johnson	189
Sarah Kwasniewski	190
Holly Woodworth	191

St John Fisher & Thomas More RC High School

Stephanie Swift	191
Helen Shoesmith	192

Eleanor Harris	192
Frances Later	193
Karina Rawlinson	194
Claire Donnelly	195
Emma Bradshaw	195
Danielle Wyld	196
Sally O'Regan	197
Laura Colvin	197
Adam Grant	198
Rebecca Villiers	199
Charlotte Bradshaw	199
Michael Bann	200
Vicky Real	200
Joey-Lee Deehan	201
Sharron Connor	201
Louise Coates	202
Steven Fenwick	202
Amanda Brennan	203
Theresa Bean	203
Stephanie Briggs	204
Heather Morrison	204
Matthew Perry	205
Martin Eyre	205
Emily Armas	206
Damien Phillips	206
Samantha Butterworth	207
Adrian Iannazzo	207
Joanne Smith	208
Lisa McDermott	208
Daniel Pitman	209
Philip Atkinson	209
Adam Palmer	210
Angela Wallwork	210
Richard Thornton	211
Emma Dundon	211
Emma-Louise Goddard	212
James Tanner	212
Victoria Ormerod	213

Simon Robert Hewitt	213
Nicola McCaigue	214
Beki Wilkinson	214
Thomas Morrison	215
Rachael Schofield	215
Maria Mendola	216
Sandra Gwinnett	216
Stephen Wademan	217
Victoria Hargreaves	218
Gemma McCaigue	219
Anna Walsh	220
Stephen James Kennedy	220
Sally Marshall	221
Charlotte Hind	222
Stephanie Sharples	222
Lisa Robinson	223
Lauren Haigh	223
Andrew Waterhouse	224
Michael Greenwood	224
Rebecca Owen	225
Katherine Dickinson	226
Jon Green	227
Alistair Eccles	228
Kate Sophia Targett	229

Saddleworth School

Bradley Whitehead	230
Tom Barrow	231
Tom Sweet	232
Karen Nicholls	233
Victoria Stothard	234
Katie Bradley	235
Leah Moore	236
Jessica Davies	237
Hugh Caffrey	238
Marisa Hill	239
Daniel Parkes	240

The Radclyffe School

Luke Higgins	241
Sarah Hilton	242
Timothy Drane	243
Aslam Amin	244
David Lepton Pulo	245
Lynette Greenwood	246
Joanne Smith	247

Walton High School

Stephen Astin	248
Cheryl Howarth	249

Wardle High School

Gemma Doodson	250
Kirsty Plumb	251
Charlotte Wilkin	252
Sarah Dean	253
Samantha Powers	254
Helen Bollington	254
Jane Edmondson	255
Kristopher Welsh	256
Kimberley Haigh	257
Ruth Harwood	258
Lisa Sarasini	259

Westleigh High School

Christine Robinson	260
Melanie Jackson	260
Allan Munro	261

THE BLUES

Someone tell me is this life?
With all the trouble and the strife
I understand, I am no fool
Why is life always so cruel?
There is no realm of understanding
And life is always so demanding
Always on the smallest side
Want to cry, but it hurts your pride
There is no shoulder there for crying
All that hurt, deceit and lying,
I am but a helpless soul
As helpless as a new born foal
Life demands you all year round
Running you into the ground
Worries you until you're tired
Mocks you down, so uninspired
Sulk and wish troubles away
Hoping better for next day.
Until next trouble you will find
Roam around, try to unwind
The troubles might be gone tomorrow
Then comes the hardest test, the sorrow
Apologies are the next stages
You could be waiting though . . .
For ages.

Paul O'Sullivan (15) Albany High School

ENVIRONMENT

What are we doing to this once beautiful world
We act as if we just don't care
To stand and watch it wither and die,
We can't let this happen but no-one will try.

Once these beautiful creatures prowled,
Now all they do is wine and howl
Because hunters, gunmen, farmers too
Are killing these animals we once knew.

The trees so tall stand peacefully
As beautiful as they can be
But not for long now we are here
Because lots of trees have disappeared.

Why has this happened, we all know why
Because no-one will bother and no-one will try
We'd better hurry up because soon it will be too late
We shouldn't have let it get to this terrible state.

Helen Fairhurst (13) Albany High School

FREEDOM

I long for the hills
I long for the trees
I long for the soft, cool mountain breeze
But most of all I long to be free.

The heathers of the moors
The crispness of the stream
The moodiness of the sea
All reminds me of being free.

Catherine Houghton (14) Albany High School

2

MY BABY BROTHER

One morning off my mother rushed,
She was puffing and panting, her hair wasn't brushed,
Eventually when she returned home,
There was something in her arms, it looked like a gnome.
It had crinkly skin and a tiny head,
All it seemed to do was sleep in a tiny bed
Sometimes it was quiet, sometimes it was loud,
For the first few weeks it caused a big crowd,
They all went coochy coo and boo, boo, boo,
Then blew big raspberries on its tummy, ooh,
This thing it wasn't nice at first,
It was so chubby, I thought it was going to burst,
Soon I learnt it was a boy,
His name was Edward and he wasn't a toy
He grew quite soon
And said things like Dadda, Mamma, tree, balloon,
My mother told me I used to be the same
I learnt to love him and call him by name
I'm older now and so is he,
But I'll never forget that little pixie.

Elizabeth Draper (11) Albany High School

3

THE MALE SPECIES

T houghtless - that's all they are
H umilating - not half by far
E vil - time after time.

M anipulating - the control isn't mine
A nimalistic - they belong in the zoo
L azy - they do nothing for you
E ffrontery - so cheeky, so rude.

S exist - they ought to be sued
P atronizing - they make us feel small
E xasperating - they make us shout and bawl
C omplicated - they come without instructions
I ncapable - of doing anything themselves
E gocentric - never a thought for the woman
S arcastic - that's all they are.

Victoria Danify (15) Albany High School

AUTUMN 1845

Autumn leaves fall
From the trees so tall,
They fall on the ground
Surrounding me all around.
And silently say winter is near.
Leaves knee deep,
And leaves crackle as
The wind blows
And the tree bends with the flow.
They look beautiful dressed in their dying colours.

Gerard Tod (12) Balderstone Community High School

PANDA

Panda, panda, stalking through the night,
Panda, panda, with your furry coat of black and white.

In the far east you originated,
Now for your fur you're being terminated.

How did God create such creatures
Never have I seen an animal with such features.

Eating bamboo shoots all day
When you're full, then you play.

Agonising is the word for watching you die,
When someone says you're not needed, that's a lie.

When it sees the predator, watch it hide,
Running towards the bushes, then jumping inside.

When I look at your eyes I see them gleam,
Watching you play and eat is just like a dream.

You live in a world of your own,
You never kill each other like us,
Living so peacefully and enjoying yourselves,
Until the human comes and takes your fur.

The panda runs when it gets a fright
When the predator looks for it, it's out of sight.

Panda, panda, stalking through the night,
Panda, panda, with your furry coat of black and white.

Humanyun Ashraf (14) Balderstone Community High School

5

THE AUTUMN IS HERE

Summer has gone
And autumn is here
Children are playing
Parents are shouting.

Trees turning colour
Red and golden brown
Children are crying
And some are laughing.

Foggy frosty mornings
Cold is pinching my nose
And cars squeaking past
Making a lot of noise.

Children playing on ice
And skating
Some of them are falling
And some are crying.

Ghulam Hussain (14) Balderstone Community High School

THE GIRAFFE

The giraffe's neck is long and thin,
His body curved and often slim.
His neck reaches up to a branch so high,
Picks off a leaf destined to die.
Crunch go his teeth so milky and white,
Swallows it down to a stomach like night.

Vicki Ward (11) Balderstone Community High School

MY OLD CAT

I once had a cat,
Who was stripy and fat,
He lived with me through childhood,
He loved me like mummy would.

I'd sleep on a single bed,
With my very old dirty ted,
He'd sit on my bed for a bit,
Then he would go downstairs,
And sit near the fireplace on a mat,
Curled up like a rat.

And that was my stripy old cat.

Shabnam Kauser (12) Balderstone Community High School

THE OLD MAN OF THE WEST

There was an old man of the west
Who has a very itchy vest
He gave it to his mother
Who washed it with a scrubber
Then she said you stupid little pest.

Mohd Zubair Bhutta (11) Balderstone Community High School

FOOTBALL

Football's a game
You always get the blame
Pushing and struggling
To get the ball
Falling and moaning
The team scores.

You don't play
Why did I come today
Everyone's cheering
Here comes the left winger.

Oh well what a shame
People say it's just a game
People shout, people cheer
In the end the score is clear.

Wayne Shailer (11) Balderstone Community High School

DEATH

Death is near me
It clings to me like seaweed
And never lets go.

Every breath I take
With every sound I make
Creeping closer and closer.

So now I will go
To where I think I belong
In a far away world.

Khalesa Nessa (12) Balderstone Community High School

DO NOT SUFFER IN SILENCE

Sitting alone in the playground
No friends have I yet found
Girls giggling, boys playing,
All alone I'm staying.

Suddenly I hear a voice
I have to listen I have no choice
'Oh it's you again,
Let's kick her feel the pain.'

I hear this all the time
'You fatty smelly piece of slime'
No-one knows the pain I feel
But the bruises are very real.

This time I've had enough
This has to end but it'll be tough
Help is available so they say
Any time, any day.

I should not suffer this violence
I should not suffer in silence.

Amina Begum (11) Balderstone Community High School

AGONY

Here I go
To the pain
To the drill
And the pliers
To the monster
Who pulls one tooth
And drills the other
Oh I hate the dentist!

Zaira Bi (12) Balderstone Community High School

9

THE SNOW

Look at the snow
As soft as dough
All fluffy and white
My garden is a beautiful sight.

But when I get out
It's as cold as an elephant's spout
Throwing snowballs at my friends
My snowman I'll defend.

But what is this?
The sky is bliss
The sun has come out
What about my snowman
I'll collect him with a pan.

But just look at the snow
As soft as dough
Just waiting for sun beams
To melt it,
The street gleams.

Jodie Atkins (12) Balderstone Community High School

UNTITLED

A victim of war in a
Land far away, spare me
A thought on your happy day.
No computers or bikes or TV
For me no fancy presents or turkey
Or tree. What I would like will not
Fill Santa's sack. All I would like
For Christmas is my family back.

Philip Deane (13) Balderstone Community High School

SCHOOL LIFE

It's boring at first but also gets worse
I'm fed up with it altogether
For life at school is totally boring
I have to write an essay for Art.

If only I'd time to give it my best
I'd have it done better than the rest
But there's just one thing that really bugs me
When the teacher says write ten pages.

If I get up early, but miss the bus
I've forgotten to do my homework
There's always an excuse that makes it work
That my small brown puppy ate it up.

But if she says 'Hey you that just won't do'
Then I'll say that my brother did it
But then she'll go mad and jump through the roof
What do you think . . . will she fall for it?

Tejal Chauhan (13) Balderstone Community High School

SAY PLEASE

I'll have a please sandwich cheese
No I mean a knees sandwich sees
Sorry I mean a keys sandwich please
No a please sandwich fleas
No   no
I'll have a doughnut.

Andrew Mallon (12) Balderstone Community High School

11

BURIED IN TIME

Do you remember?
When we used to sit out in the garden,
Eating soil.
And when someone would come out,
We'd hide the soil behind us.
And pretend to be playing.

Do you remember . . .
When we used to grab a chair and open
The back door,
We would ride to our granddad's factory
On our bikes.
Grandad would bring us back holding
Us by the jumpers.

Do you remember . . .
When I had my fifth birthday party,
The lights went out,
I was ready to blow the candles out.
My friend pushed my face into the cake
They switched the lights on and laughed at me.

Do you remember . . .
When we were once playing in the playground,
We all fell on top of each other
By arguing.
There was a big pile of us
How funny we looked.

I hope you will read this . . .
And remember the last threads of our childhood.

Hamara Ahmed (12) Balderstone Community High School

THE GOLDEN ACORN

There it was,
Standing there,
All alone.
In the middle of the field
The acorns dangled dazzled
And shined.
The squirrels went
Collecting them
As they nibbled on
The acorns
One of them stopped with fear.
He found these
Were gold
And went off to show the others.
They all scattered back to
The tree.
In just a few minutes
The acorns were gone
And the tree was alone
Once more.

Becky Schofield (12) Balderstone Community High School

THE DOVE

Dove white, graceful wings,
Glides over the deep blue sea.
Forever flying.

John Holt (12) Balderstone Community High School

A LETTER TO MY FRIEND

Do you remember,
When we walked together?
You told me about yourself
So then I said will you
Be my best friend?

Do you remember?
You were a joker?
To have me chase
You used to pull
A face.

Do you remember
When we wished together?
If we could stay
With each other forever
And ever.

Do you remember
When we used to share our
Secrets between each other
From home to school
We go.

Do you remember
When we used to hide in trees?
Oh those beautiful leaves

I hope you will remember all our childhood.

Nausheen Bibi (13) Balderstone Community High School

THE NEW BOY

This is the day
I've always dreaded
As I think of the things
That are in my head.

> The door swung inwards
> The boys all laughed
> When they saw
> I was the new lad.

I was pushed and shoved and
Rolled in mud
Then one boy said,
'That's no good.'

> All of a sudden
> I was left alone
> Should I run
> Or should I groan?

Then came that boy
He said 'Please don't cry'
With a smile on his face
He said 'Let's race' and
Now we're really good
Mates.

Deborah Taylor (13) Balderstone Community High School

HOMELESS FOLK

Homeless men sleeping,
In the train station begging,
Hoping they'll get food.

Paul Taylor (13) Balderstone Community High School

HOW NICE IT IS TO GO AWAY

How nice it is to go away,
On a lovely holiday.
Even though it's fun to roam,
It's even better coming home.
Coming home, coming home,
It's really lovely coming home.

It's even better on a sunny day,
When you go on a holiday.
Even though it's fun to roam,
It's even better coming home,
Coming home, coming home,
It's really lovely coming home.

Katherine Robinson (13) Balderstone Community
High School

BONFIRE NIGHT

Red hot flames, jumping.
People wrapped up to be safe.
Fireworks whiz, crack, twizz.

Vicki Louise McKenzie-Lunn (12) Balderstone Community
High School

WINTER TIME

I love the winter
The snow glistens in the sun
And the snowman melts.

Ian Sharp (12) Balderstone Community High School

MISCHIEVOUS AUTUMN LEAVES

Leaves on trees will soon be heltering,
                              Sheltering,
                    Twirling,
                              Dancing.

Downwards through the air
Until they are exhausted
And come drooping, looping down
The leaves change colour from
                    green
                    to brown
                    to red
                    to orange.

Then dry up and go brittle
Someone naughty comes and kicks
                    them
                    into
                    the
                    dull
                    grey
                    air.

Tahira Mukhtar (12) Balderstone Community High School

17

THE FIREWORK LAMENT

I was lit,
        And was sent into the dark grey sky,
But lit up by the other fireworks.
I could see all the people gazing up below.
Then I reached the sky and all went quiet,
Then I shattered into millions of colourful pieces.

Umar Saeed (11) Balderstone Community High School

SCHOOL

The children arrived.
They came in, in their hundreds
Squashing and squeezing,
Pushing and crushing,
Forcing their way through.
They squashed into registration,
And sat down and talked.
They nattered and nattered,
And chattered and chattered,
Then the teacher came in.

We got there and the teacher,
Gave us our books,
And talked about what we were doing.
History, Science, Language and Maths,
Geography,
Technology, Drama and Art,
All lessons we have every week.

Home time at last!
Crushed as you come out,
Eating sweets that have gone mouldy in your bag.

Emma Cottam (11) Balderstone Community High School

FOUNTAIN

Leaping, tinkling,
The water is falling, from
A fountain so small.

Sarah Ward (13) Balderstone Community High School

HELP ME!

My head was spinning,
My eyes shut tight,
I couldn't think,
I couldn't speak.
My temperature rising, sweat streaming down my face.
My head was thumping,
Like a time bomb wanting to explode
Boom, boom, my heart was beating fast.
I wanted to scream, I wanted to shout
'Help me!' 'Help me!'
But I couldn't, I could barely breathe.
Then suddenly silence, the thunderous beating of my
Heart gone.
I lay there cold, lifeless, dead.
And what for? What was it all for?
To be one of the gang,
To have a bit of a laugh,
How stupid could I have been, what a fool I was,
LSD was definitely not for me.

Qumar Mahmud (14) Balderstone Community High School

AUTUMN

Autumn the season of wonder
Comes once a year at the time of September
A time when trees lose their cover.
Leaves changing colour to colour
Red, orange, green and finally yellow
Fall to the ground with colourful mellow.
Children running in the parks
Kicking the leaves, fun and laughs
Squirrels running finding shelter
Collecting nuts in search of food
Birds, badgers, hedgehogs too,
Mother, father, children too
Curl up together to sleep the hibernation
                    through.

Naveed Haaris Sahraouei (11) Balderstone Community
High School

SNAKES

The snake glides slowly out of its holes.
Living rope a metre long
Blackish deadly with a poisonous bite
The snake lay at its tree trunk
I saw it moving, its skin
Polished in the sun.
Terrified, I ran
It was awake at night
And give me a fright.

Basharat Hussain (14) Balderstone Community High School

THE FOUR SEASONS

The summer sunshine
Shines above us all day long
After falls the rain.

In the autumn field
I walk through the crunchy leaves
After blows the wind.

White snow on a field
The whiteness in the background
Shows up the bare trees.

Spring buds opening
The colourful flowers show
Whilst the tree leaves grow.

Doliz Miah (13) Balderstone Community High School

DOLPHIN

Dolphin, dolphin in the sea
With its friends all the time.

Very clever, very fast
When it sees a big shark it swims into the dark.

When the storm and lightning comes
They flee in dread
Dolphin dive down to the bottom sea bed.

When the sun comes up on the warm black sea
Dolphin come up and play in security.

Nadeem Tariq (14) Balderstone Community High School

MYSTICAL SEA

Sea, deep, dark, magic
Home to fish, dolphins and crabs
Holds many wonders.

Jody Margerison (13) Balderstone Community High School

THE WITCH

Flying high, soaring into the sky
Silhouetted in the moonlight
Hair streaked out behind her
Chanting her evil deeds.

Faster she zoomed around the world
Putting everyone under her spell
Hypnotising them with her eyes
Prancing on another victim.

Till the world was helpless at her feet
To listen to her every command
Fufilling her strange wishes
Until there was nothing left to wish for.

One fatal mistake she made so soon
To own the moon, to possess the stars
No-one could manage this impossible task
So in a fit of rage she cast her spell.

When it just seemed within her reach
The power of her wish just was too strong
With an explosive bang she burst into smoke
And disappeared from the earth forever.

Monwara Begum (15) Balderstone Community High School

I ONCE SAW . . .

I once saw a weird animal,
Walking down my street.
He had a very furry coat,
And a lot of meat.

He went around the corner
And then behind the bush
He saw his wife behind it
And came out in a rush.

He ran back around the corner,
And back up the busy street
I once saw a weird animal
Running up my street.

Tahira Akhtar (13) Balderstone Community High School

MY BOYFRIEND GAVE ME AN APPLE

My boyfriend gave me an apple
My boyfriend gave me a pear
My boyfriend gave me a kiss on the lips
So I kicked him down the stairs
I kicked him over Sunderland
I kicked him over France
I kicked him over Blackpool Tower
And he lost his underpants.

Mannié A (12) Balderstone Community High School

A PERFECT WORLD

I could sit in a room all alone.
No light, no world, nobody.
Just on my own
No worries, no hurries
No lies, no cries
No-one's rules, no-one's cruel.
Just me floating in bubbles
Staying out of trouble
It wouldn't be a perfect world.

To love and care
For old and young to share
Take every chance
Low and high
Don't turn around and wave goodbye
When you know it's worth a try
Take it in pride
The world is on your side
It wouldn't be a perfect world
Without no love, no you,
No me, no world.

Nighat Kauser (13) Balderstone Community High School

HEAVEN

Up there amongst the clouds and sun.
With melons and peaches and lots of buns.
Where no-one goes to bed till late,
And history books are out of their date.
That's the land to which I will go.
You push a button and down comes the snow.

Joanne Burgess (12) Balderstone Community High School

FAR AWAY

In my eyes tears begin to fall,
When I remember her,
How can I go and tell her,
How much she upset me.

In my heart I have a picture of her,
I was worried about why she left,
Is it because she loved me?
Or is it because she cared?

There's only one girl for me,
And that's her
I would like to go and tell her
But she's gone
Gone as far as she can
Was she afraid
Or was she just playing games.

She's the one I want,
Just her,
Not anyone else,
Just her,

Come back soon,
For my sake.

Naz K (14) Balderstone Community High School

IT'S NOT FAIR!

It's not fair!
Why do I feel lonely
It's not fair why I'm the one and only,
I have to be selfish
Because I'm the one to blame all
The time.
I try to clear my feelings out,
But instead I get shouted at
And told to be quiet.

I'm confused because of this
Obnoxious world.
It treats me like it's found dirt!

I try to express myself,
But then I don't have the
Confidence to tell a soul.

I'm starting to feel I'm lonely
Living a big fat lie!
I only wished to be noticed and
Cared for, where is this love,
Is it hidden behind trapped
Flowers.

I'm scared!
My open fears will turn into
Hidden fears.

I'm like a flower which is
Losing all its sensitivity and the
Fresh smell,

I try to continue to live,
Like a normal girl because I want
To feel consulted!

Shaista Kauser (14) Balderstone Community High School

26

GRAVEYARD

Each dared each other to turn up on that night
Some came on foot some came by bike.
No-one said a single word.
The only sound from a passing bird.
They all sat together each on a stone
But they might as well have been there each alone
Each sat there no knowing what to expect
Sat there each an awful wreck.
Once the silence had been broken
And each person had spoken
They all had to try and boast
But then someone asked do you believe
In ghosts?
Someone answered yes
This person said that he reckoned there
Was a ghost behind having a rest
They all turned about.
Each of them had some doubt
They all found out it was a hoax
Who did he think he was telling a joke
They sat there all relaxed
No-one saw what was behind their backs
It was a spirit from the dead
Sat there on its own grave bed
The spirit did not need to move
Suddenly no-one had anything to prove.

Emma Williams (14) Balderstone Community High School

PEACE

Why do people have to fight?
What's the point in having a war?
Why do so many people have to die
To try and prove who's best?
Why do guns have to rage across the land,
And bullets fly across the sky?
Can somebody tell me the reason why?

Why do people have to suffer,
Because their leaders disagree?
Why can't these 'great men' stop and think,
Before destroying half the land?
When will the day of peace arise?
Oh somebody tell me when?

Gemma Lee (12) Balderstone Community High School

THE CRICKET WORLD CUP FINAL

I feel uneasy watching the match,
Biting my nails and rattling my teeth,
The team was in a bad situation,
I felt like turning the TV off,
But gradually they recovered,
I feel a small particle of the whole match,
As 9 billion fans watch the match,
The cornered tigers fight and fight,
Emotion covers the living room
As Pakistan win the World Cup.

Israr Hussain (15) Balderstone Community High School

POLLUTION

What has the world done to you?
Has it eaten you up?
Thrown you in outer space?
Spat on you?
Sat on you?
Or called you names?

Has the world had a fight with you?
Had an argument?
Killed you?
Damaged you?
Or shouted at you for walking on it?

Has the world said get lost?
Get off me,
Don't touch me,
Don't walk on me,
Or don't build anymore on me?

Has the world told you off?
Scolded you?
Frightened,
Scared,
Or hurt you?

> Then why do you,
> Drop litter,
> Spoil the atmosphere,
> Pollute the waters,
> And many other things?

What I don't understand,
Is why you do all this.
These are questions I need answers for.

Shabana Anwar (12) Balderstone Community High School

TIME BOMB

Flowing like a river,
Life goes on.
Violence and poverty,
Abuse and cruelty.
Ships swaying across the sea,
Ready for a battle.
'IRA' and Iraqi squad,
Bombing all the land,
Life is like a
Time bomb ready to go off!

Susan Garvey (12) Balderstone Community High School

DRUGS, SEX AND ROCK AND ROLL

Drugs, sex and rock and roll.
Fantasies of many since they were ten years old.

Sex is reproduction with extreme sensual production.
Drugs are for mugs who behave like thugs.
The addiction alone has destroyed many,
While robbing them for every penny.

Rock and roll has topped every pole
Even rocked foxes from their hole.
The powerful beat when left alone
Is stronger than Sylvester Stallone.

Who needs drugs, sex and rock and roll.
When you can go to the park for a quiet stroll.

Zia Uddin (15) Balderstone Community High School

DREAM OR REALITY?

It was a day of fear, terror and scream
Oh! If only it was a nightmarish dream.
As I stood in a pit of blood
I had a distinctive look of consternation
As I felt a queer sensation
Throughout my body, throughout my soul
An anathema entwining my mind.
It gathered in like an elaborate sin
'Oh! What has this creature done to me within?'
Its deary grasp became inextricable to me
My only thought became 'break free, break free!'
A strange combination of a mixed, queer sensation
Made me feel the creature's eminence,
Confluenting into my body.
Then it became clear to see
The creature was switching minds with me.
I tried to block its power from my head
But its mind pull became harder instead.
I tried to think of happy memories, of times well spent
But the creature's pull wouldn't repent.
I could feel my body getting further away
Then I shouted 'Get off me, get away!'
My mind became full of menacing rage.
I could feel my body being pulled to a familiar state.
My body and soul were becoming whole again.
Then in an instant the creature was gone
I became baffled, I'd just escaped fate
Was it an illusion, could it have been a dream?
One thing is for certain
I remember my scream!

Julie Jones (14) Balderstone Community High School

31

REVENGE

In the depths of forest,
Late at night.
The tomb door sprung open,
And he stepped out.
He was tall and sinister,
Dark and secretive.
His eyes were full of revenge.
For what he had waited for,
Waited so long, was revenge.

In his bed, all cosy and warm,
Was the man.
The murderer who,
Got away with it.
He got drunk, drunk and angry,
And chased the deceased.
Cornered him and in cold blood,
Murdered him.
The murderer fled,
Leaving him for dead, lying all alone.
Alone, afraid and cold.

His family grief stricken,
Laid him to rest, in the forest,
His favourite place,
But now he has stirred, awakened
And crazed,
Thirsty for blood!

For the murderer,
The night will be long.
For there's nowhere to hide and,
Nowhere to run, from,
Revenge!

Emma Patterson (15) Balderstone Community High School

FOREVER

The creaking of the rocking chair,
Has something sinister in its sound.
The small girl who slumbers in it,
Weeps in time to the creaks.

The small girl was not human,
All people around believed this fact.
The devilish atmosphere,
Was certainly a clue.

There was no mother or father in sight,
So something was extremely weird.
A fierce look spread across her face,
Maybe she killed her parents, who knows.

Most people loathed the ghastly odour,
That toured the atrocious blood filled rooms.
This could be a clue to the whereabouts
Of her mystery parents.

There never was parents,
She wasn't human, just guts and gore.
An eternal soul
That would roam forever more.

Claire Cocker (15) Balderstone Community High School

DEATH

It creeps in, at the happiest time of your life
Under the door, through the cracks in the floor.
No-one can escape it.

It carries you away in the twinkling of an eye,
Or if it is not you,
Your friends and family.

Swiftly it comes,
No-one knows, whence and where it comes.
Some day 'hell' and some 'heaven'.

Its chariot is swift,
As swift as a bird.
A lone black horse with plumes,
Pulls the black cart.
Slowly they march,
With the sombre coachman.

The air is chill, but still,
The atmosphere could be cut with a knife.

It is only a step behind you,
And everyone you know.
It will tap you on the shoulder,
And if you turn around,
It will take you away.

Chanine Harris (14) Balderstone Community High School

ETERNAL SPIRITS

The ghosts, the spirits, the screams of pain
They were all in the film again.
The gasps from the crowds as they saw all the blood
But Katy and Adam both thought it was good
The noise was so loud, each sound made them shake
They'd sit in their chairs and together they'd quake
But then all of a sudden, out of the blue
Katy and Adam didn't know what to do
They were swirling, tumbling and moving around
Their frightening scream was the only sound
There were flashing lights of red, blue and green
Katy and Adam had been sucked into the screen
Then quick as a flash, they were in another land
Both of them had a gun in their hand
And lying beneath them was the body of a boy
In a pool of blood that covered his toy
They were the spirits of the men of death
Who had taken away their victim's breath
Then there was the siren, the flashing blue light
Wherever they looked, they were always in sight
The police ran towards them, pushed them against a wall
Handcuffed them both and searched them all
They went off in the car and were both sent to jail
Neither of them were granted bail
It must now be very plain to see
They were the spirits for eternity.

Suzanne Cliffe (15) Balderstone Community High School

THE OTHER WORLD

The world of dreams
Where anything is possible.
Wild adventures are unparalleled
But when reality creeps in, euphoria dies.
Life returns to its mediocre - self.

The realm of nightmares,
Where the possible and impossible exist.
Adventures turn black, chaos takes hold,
Paranoia, insecurity and bewilderment.

Nightmares can wait,
Like an imprint in your sub-concious,
They can return.
Fear is my drug, and it can manifest, metamorphose
And seep into ordinary reality.

The nightmare is my reality,
And the blanket of fear is my shroud.
I am the needle in your vein,
I am the macabre you can't sustain.

I am nightmare.

Karen Whittles (15) Balderstone Community High School

36

MY BIKE

Christmas came and my mum asked
Me,
'What would I like.'
I quickly answered I would like a mountain bike.
Christmas morning came and my dreams came true.
For there it was big, bright and blue.
I rushed opening the rest of my presents
Because I wanted to go for a ride.
I rolled down my socks and took it outside
I pedalled down the road on that very morning
When a car pulled out without any
Warning I crashed and fell on the floor
Now my bike is under the stairs
Forever more.

Kelly Gray (13) Balderstone Community High School

WAR

Sounds of machine guns, echoed in the air,
The cries of the people made my heart bleed.
Children all around us can't see the need,
To fight with each other anymore.

Young fathers, brothers leave their homes,
To fight with the enemy on the war front,
Mother, sister alone at home,
Counting the days for when they'll come home.

I don't see why, people have to fight,
To show who's right or wrong,
Why can't we live in a peaceful world,
Altogether in harmony and love.

Nadia Sultana (15) Balderstone Community High School

TRAPPED

There was a loud bang
Everything went black,
I knew I was trapped
And there was no way back.

The dust began to choke me
There was nothing I could do,
I just lay there and prayed
That somebody knew.

There was another crash
And the earth shook,
The coal began to tumble
But all I could do was look.

I heard voices outside
I began to shout,
I yelled, 'Help I'm in here
And I can't get out.'

The roof began to leak
It was raining outside,
What I wouldn't do
To get out alive.

The air became thin
I thought I would die,
There was nothing I could do
I began to cry.

All I could think of was dying
What would happen to my wife?
She would be all alone
God, I need my life!

Jaclyn Bell (15) Balderstone Community High School

TICK, TICK, TICK, TOCK

Tick, tick, tick, tock,
I look up and I see the clock.
What! It's already that time?
Oh my God, I hope I do fine,
I look up at the next question, what does it mean?
I haven't got a clue and I think I'm gonna scream.

Tick, tick, tick, tock,
What is that noise? It's that damn clock!
I can't see the questions, my eyes are blurred,
I don't know what I'm doing, but I feel like such a nerd.
What was it that my mother had said?
Don't panic, take deep breaths and always keep your head.

Tick, tick, tick, tock,
Once I get my grades I'm going to have a big shock,
Right! Three deep breaths I will take,
And do my best for my own sake.
If I don't know the answers I'll make them up,
And I won't care if I get stuck.

Tick, tick, tick, tock,
I'm sure there's something wrong with that clock.
What's that the teacher's saying?
What only fifteen minutes to go, I think I better start praying.
Hang on! I know the answers to these,
Ten minutes left, oh do let me finish please.

Tick, tick, tick, tock,
Thank you God for that clock,
I'm sure I've done well,
Even though it felt like going through hell.

Ambar Rashid (16) Balderstone Community High School

39

ADOLESCENCE!

My life it seems is such a bore
Just an everlasting chore
'Wash the pots', 'Make a brew'
Like I've got nothing else to do.
I'd rather be out having a laugh
Filing my nails, taking a bath
But no, my homework must come first
There's too much, I'm gonna burst
I can't wait till exams are done
Then I can relax and have some fun!

Carly Welsh (15) Balderstone Community High School

UNDER THE EARTH

As I lie under the soil,
Creatures squirm,
Pressure boils.

No-one's here,
It's gone dark,
Wooden box,
Made of bark.

Death has slowly come upon me,
Relations grieve,
Let them be.

Coffin hard,
Nothing left,
Rotting away,
Handling death.

Cheryl Anne McKenna (16) Balderstone Community High
School

THE NEW WORLD

There will come a time when evil rules
When the land is filled with goblins and ghouls.

Hatred will linger upon the air
Monsters will murder without a care.

Vampires and trolls abuse magical powers
The world as we knew it is no longer ours.

The goodness, banished into the night
The universe left a gruesome sight.

We are left instead with unbearable pain
Our hopes disappeared like tears into rain.

Catherine McManus (15) Balderstone Community
High School

FIREWORK NIGHT

Fireworks are fun to watch,
Streaming through the sky,
Red, orange, green and blue,
Illuminate people passing by.
Treacle toffee, cakes and sweets,
People eat all night.
Catherine wheels and bangers too.
Give people pleasant frights.
Then it's time to pack away,
And go back to our homes,
But before that happens,
We must burn,
Guy Fawkes in the fire and wood.

Stephen Russell (13) Balderstone Community High School

THE GREEK'S BELIEF

This is how it all began
This is how the world started.
First there was nothing, only chaos, the void,
But then its clinging mists parted
To reveal a single celestial form
Gaea was born, Mother Earth,
The very first of the Goddesses
And to Uranus the sky God she gave birth.

They married and Gaea bore children
But Uranus was heartless and cruel.
He banished the Cyclopes to the Underworld
So Cronos, his son, did with him duel.
Cronos, a Titan mighty and strong
With a sickle took Uranus' life.
Triumphant, he became king of the Titans
And took his sister Rhea as his wife.

Warned he would be slain by his child
Cronos swallowed each tiny bundle of flesh and bone,
Not knowing that for the last one
Outraged, Rhea had substituted a stone.
Zeus, last born freed his siblings
And against Cronos led a revolt.
He freed the Cyclopes and with their help
Killed Cronos with a thunderbolt.

Zeus now became King of the Gods
To his brother, Poseidon, he gave the Ocean and seas,
To his sister Hera, his hand in marriage,
To Pluto the Underworld, Hades.
To this very day our Gods rule still
They always have and they always will.

Gillian Hinds (16) Balderstone Community High School

VOICES

As I stand alone I hear a sound,
Something joyful, something loud,
Something beating, something drumming,
The sound of music.

The sound grows distant,
The sound wears out.
The joy and beating fade away.
The sound of silence.

The sound seems different
More happy and quaint
Not loud nor silent
Just the sound of singing.

The sound becomes louder,
More friendly and loving
More speaking than singing
This is the sound of words!

Nicola Hall (14) Balderstone Community High School

TEEN SPIRIT

Teen spirit, what does that mean?
Both genders trying to be seen.
As not as bad as they think,
But who are they, and what do they see?

Just do it, just do it, just do it for me,
And let them all really see,
How bad you are,
How far you'll go.
Then you're threatened with trouble
Hey, so?

I've done it once, I'll do it again,
But I don't mean to be a pain.
It gives me lots of attention,
Regardless of apprehension.
So do you see, what's happened
To me?
Please don't blame our generation.

Mike Stapleton (14) Balderstone Community High School

ZODIAC

Now I am a scorpion,
Creeping through the night,
Giving people a fright,
Killing them and eating them.

I felt this sudden urge to kill,
To kill a human.
I was out in the dark night
And I could sense his fright.

This urge to kill is growing,
Throwing me out of line.
I didn't have much time,
I needed to get home.

Now he was here,
I pounced out and stung his ear,
He cried out with a scream
And hit the ground with a thud!

Dawn is nearly here,
I was making my way home,
Hoping to sleep in my cosy dome.

I lay down feeling tired,
When I woke up the next morning,
I felt myself falling . . .

Cheryl Hill (15) Balderstone Community High School

DOLPHINS

Dolphins are such playful creatures
Why do we kill them so?
All they do is play and eat
And look at cute as they can be.
Yet we kill them and not even for their meat.

The sea is their home and they come up to breathe,
Yet all fishermen kill them with greed,
They say they eat the fish
But what more can they feed upon
When the fishermen take their food.

How cruel we can be
Without seeing what they mean.
Dolphins are such playful creatures
Why do we hurt them so?
Kill them, beat them and hit them like they are savage
Beasts.

Ashyia Rafique (13) Balderstone Community High School

THE LAST GOODBYE

A bird cries in the distance, the sun sets in the sky,
The moon comes out to greet me, I wave one last goodbye.

I feel so tired and lonely, my heart's began to crack,
I just cannot believe, he's never coming back.

The questions are continuous, the things I've said and done,
Would things be very different, if the row had not begun?

It's too late now to change things, there's no reason left to try,
There's nothing I can do, I've no tears left to cry.

If only I could change all the things I've said,
If only fate had passed him, and taken me instead.

There's no use now in lying, deep inside I know,
My torment will be endless, my guilt will never go.

Maria Beadsworth (13) Balderstone Community High School

WAR

Over the world
Rages war.

Bosnia, Rwanda and Iraq

All this happens very fast
When the bombs come down and nothing lasts.

Millions are dead
Why couldn't they talk instead?

People are crying, it's very sad
Others are trying not to be bad.

Looking for peace in the Middle East
Yitzhak Shamir and Yassir Arafat negotiate.

Proving that it is never too late.

Nowhere to go, nowhere to hide
Just like always the politicians lied.

Muhammad Irfan (15) Balderstone Community High School

PEACE PLEASE

The world is in trouble,
There's crime all around,
The rain forests are dying a death.
There's fighting and killing
And suffering and pain,
Not to mention the wars and the rest.

It all has to end,
This old morbid trend,
For the good of the people on earth.
The fighting must stop
The crime rate must drop
And we should teach the right values from birth.

United be proud,
Let your voices be loud,
So they're heard by the people in power.
But it's not just us people,
It's our environment too,
So look after each plant and each flower.

So put down your guns
Your chainsaws and knives,
And let the peace movement begin.
United we stand,
Divided we fall
And together we'll eventually win.

Andrew Blackshaw (15) Balderstone Community
High School

THE NIGHT

The night is dark and lonely,
The skies are dark and bleak,
The winds are blowing fully
As we hear the owls shriek.
You kept saying you loved me,
We ended up kissing all night.
I only want you to see
What I'm like when I'm cheery and bright.
When the sunset came out
A smile rose upon my face.
I heard the children shout,
As raindrops came down like lace.
The morning ended sadly,
As we said our good-byes,
We wanted this so badly,
To be happy the rest of our lives.

Lisa Critchley (15) Beardwood School

ANIMAL EXPERIMENTS

Animal testing is it good or bad?
A lot of people think it's sad,
That animals suffer for our needs
And we live our lives at ease.
Do we realise the pain they go through
Or is it just we don't really want to?
Animals placed in little cages
Unaware of the dangers,
But as the time starts ticking by.
Another little animal has to die.
But at the end of the day we have to say
Who has the right to take a life away?

Mary Davidson (12) Beardwood School

NATURE

Nature is not just a bird, tree or water,
Nature is what you can see, feel or hear.

Nature is everything around you,
You don't have to search for nature,
Nature is within you, within your reach.

Come to the nature, feel the nature and love the nature.

Mandee Corkin (13) Beardwood School

WINTER TIME

Cold and frosty mornings
Shivering, freezing nights
More earlier it gets darker
The less we have of light.

Snow is lying everywhere
Twigs and branches here and there
Some snowmen being built
Some people are lying on quilts.

Staying inside
With the fire blazing
Having hot cocoa
Nothing to do amazing.

Now winter has gone away
And spring has come
Enjoy the weather
With a lot of fun!

Tubassum Asghar (12) Beardwood School

BORING OLD ENGLISH

I absolutely hate the lesson English
I'd rather be with a dead, smelly fish.

Speech marks, commas, full stops etc
Make me go crazy altogether.

If a mistake is made whilst reading a book
The teacher will give a disappointing look.

If work gets a little messy,
The teacher shouts 'Do it again and get busy.'

Having to learn writing by Shakespeare,
What an ancient task, oh dear, oh dear.

Oh I really hate that lesson English,
I wish it would simply vanish.

Shabana Hussain (12) Beardwood School

AUTUMN TIME

Autumn is here now
Leaves are changing colours
And falling off the branches.
They are swirling in the wind
And crispy as I walk through.
Christmas is near and it will
Start getting cold
But I don't care, soon it will be warm again
And things will start to grow.
Animals will begin to appear
The babies will begin to play
The breeze is pleasant
Warm sun will beat down
The sky will be clear.

Avril Hardman (16) Beaumont College

SPRING

My favourite season of the year
Is spring because I always hear
The sweet and clear song of birds,
And see the fields full of herds.
Spring too is a season for new life,
Baby animals are born and growth becomes rife.
There are lots of new and fresh smells too,
From flowers and plants to grasses and dew.
I also like the colours of flowers,
They brightly shine out in April showers,
Also the new leaves soft and green,
Make this season so serene.

Michelle Lund (13) Carr Hill High School

WINTER

Walking home from my school
Boys and girls acting the fool
Hat and scarf around my neck
Starting to snow what the heck.

Snow falling on the ground
Looking white all around
Girls running having fun
Hope we don't have any sun.

Building a snowman out the back
Nose of carrot, eyes so black
What to use for his teeth
Lips above and underneath.

Snow is melting getting sad
Snowman melted that we had
Sun is shining for another day
Winter's going, spring's on its way.

Donna Bates (12) Carr Hill High School

AUTUMN

Autumn leaves falling down,
Red, yellow and brown,
People scuffling through the leaves,
Also listening to the autumn breeze.

Look here come the dark clouds,
'There's going to be a storm,' someone shouts
Out loud.
First there were thunderbolts and then the
Lightning.
People think this is frightening.

Trees shake and windows rattle,
Then the wind joins in on this battle,
Leaves swirl round and round,
While the grass clings to the ground.

The leaves swirl down and down,
Now only the rain pelts against the ground,
The people are listening for the rain,
While they're safe inside behind the pane.

Matthew Baker (12) Carr Hill High School

THE CORNER SHOP

The corner shop is my favourite place
I go there quite a lot
The shopkeeper has a friendly face
He's funny and laughs a lot.

My favourite sweets are aniseed balls
Mints and chocolate too!
Sweets cover all the walls
The counter is full too!

There are many visitors -
Polly, Pam and Sue
Mr and Mrs Turnbull
There always is a queue.

So if you're ever passing by
Come in and try the sweets
You'll never be unwelcome so
Come treat yourself to sweets.

Sarah Wright (12) Carr Hill High School

THE MONSTER

Everyone says monsters are fake
But I saw one by the lake
Honest I did.
I'm sure it was eating a kid
It was big and green, slimy and red
One step nearer I could have been dead
It also had spots
And big blue dots
It glared at me
Thinking there's my tea
Licking its lips
Drooling over its red hot grips
I backed away and got down on my
Knees and started to pray
I rushed towards a cave
Now I wasn't being brave
I got to the end of it and found a great big massive pit
I jumped and there I was at the bottom of it
All I could do was sit
I heard a roar
And there was the monster at the little door
I ran and ran
And saw a very old man
The monster stopped and turned around
The reason for that will never come round.

Cassandra Goodes (12) Carr Hill High School

THE THING UNDER THE STAIRS

I'm sure there's something under the stairs
Could it be a couple of bears?
It could even be a musical thing
I hear it shout and dance and sing.
I've taken a look and had a few peeks
I can't see nothin' and the cupboard reeks
It could be green and large and hairy
And I'm sure if I saw it, I'd think it was scary.

I've told my mum and I've told my dad
But they don't believe me and they think I'm mad
Tonight I'm going to go down there
Step by step and stair by stair
I'm going to see what this thing is
If it's got hair or if it's got zits.
You never know it might not be much
But it could turn you to stone with just a touch.
But then again I might not look
Instead at night I'll read a book.

Sophie Cunningham (12) Carr Hill High School

LIFE GOES ON

I saw what I shouldn't have,
Gasped with pain,
Ran and ran far away,
My heart beat faster,
My hands stretched out,
Searching for the person I could never
Live without.

Far on in years,
Experience great,
The pain I felt,
Is no more my fate,
It's locked away,
Deep inside,
A part of my life I will always hide.

Now as I look back,
I see my fear,
Isolated,
No-one came near,
I coped alone,
Pushed my way through,
Drowning in the pain and sorrow
I once knew,
But I know now
What I didn't then,
Life goes on,
Through the pain,
And somehow, I've learnt to live again.

Zoë Bell (15) Crompton House School

SEASONS

Summer is the best time of year,
School is out holidays are here,
Children shouting Hooray! Hooray!
Come out and enjoy the day.

Spring is the season for Easter bunnies,
With lots of lovely tasty honey,
With blossoming trees,
And lots of new born buzzing bees.

Autumn is the season for leaves turning red,
Leaves falling down all over they shed,
Spinning-jennies all over the sky and ground,
And the twigs cracking what a sound.

Winter is the season for snow,
Nobody has ever felt so low,
With Christmas carols and Christmas trees,
All over the world joy and peace.

Naila Nisar (13) Darwen Moorland High School

PEOPLE

People here, people there,
People are almost everywhere,
Everybody all around,
People in the air, people on the ground,
People in ships, people in cars,
People on the moon, people on Mars,
People in factories, people who keep bumble bees,
People black, people white,
All these people are all alike.

Laura Farran (12) Darwen Moorland High School

IN MY HEAD

In my head I see a nice lad waving,
In my head I see a patch of mud,
In my head I hear a little lad crying,
In my head I only wish I could.

In my head I see Andre' Agassi,
In my head I see a tennis ball
In my head I see an Intercity train
In reality I want them all.

In my head I see chicken and chips,
The things I long to eat
In my head I think I'll have them for tea
Instead of a plate of meat.

In my head I see a teacher thinking
Of all the things we could do today.
She chose maths, my worst lesson
If only it was yesterday.

Elizabeth Taylor (13) Darwen Moorland High School

ALONE

She has taken out the candle
She has left me in the dark
From the window not a glimmer
From the fireplace not a spark.

I am frightened as I'm lying
All alone in my bed
And I've wrapped the clothes so
Closely
As I can around my head.

But what is it that makes me tremble
And why should I fear the gloom
I am certain there is nothing
In the corners of the room.

Alex Hannon (13) Darwen Moorland High School

WHAT MISS?

I walked into a classroom
What was I going to say?
I hadn't done the homework
That was given yesterday.
I walked into the classroom
I quietly shut the door
I sat down at my table
And the teacher I'd ignore.
The teacher came to my desk
She put her hand on my head.
You haven't done your homework so
You can do this work instead.

Kirsty Ure (14) Darwen Moorland High School

WHY DAD?

Why do people grow dad?
Why do people die?
Why do people smile dad?
Why do people cry?
Why do people run dad?
Why do people walk?
Why are people silent dad?
Why do people talk?
Why do people sleep dad?
Why do some stay awake?
Why do we have legs dad?
Why do some of them break?
Why do people marry dad?
Why do some split up?
Why do people kill dad?
And mess their whole life up?

Mathew Banks (14) Darwen Moorland High School

IN MY HEAD . . .

In my head,
There is a monster,
And it scares the hell out of me,
When I am alone in bed.
Suddenly,
Shadows become fearful creatures,
Lurking in every corner,
Waiting,
Pouncing when I dare move.
Then I blink,
And I realise,
That it is just my imagination again.

Nicola Dinsdale (13) Darwen Moorland High School

THE TEDDY BEAR

There is a teddy in the corner of your room
This teddy feels sad with tears and full of gloom.
This teddy has had its eyes pulled out
And all his fluff has gone.
But all his friend, you, has done is buy
Another one.
It lies there thinking of his old teddy
Life.
He's been stabbed a hundred times by his
Friend's army knife.
But then he jumps up feeling really mad.
He puts on his Rambo suit and makes
Himself look bad.
He puts on a head lamp and machine gun
Too.
He shoots another teddy and makes them
Cry boo, hoo.
He beats up all my figures and army men
I like. He knocks the Terminator off and does
A wheely on his bike.
But now it's day and it starts to get light
Now the night is over and so is the fight.

Westley Pickup (13) Darwen Moorland High School

I'M AFRAID I HAVEN'T GOT MY HOMEWORK

I'm afraid I haven't got my homework Miss,
But I've got a good excuse today.
I mean, yesterday's about the custard was a bit of a lie Miss.

Well, it was a bit exaggerated anyway.
You see, what happened last night was, my homework
                              grew legs and then it ran away!

It's all my brother's fault, he's been playing with his
                                   chemistry set again.
It wasn't acid though, this time Miss, it was a potion
                              that reacts with the rain.
He poured this potion on my homework, you see,
And it was then that the hurricane came.

Of course the roof was ripped off our house Miss,
So there was a massive rush of rain.
My homework grew legs and ran away Miss,
Never to be seen again!

Claire Dean (13) Darwen Moorland High School

MY DOG

When I was three,
I got a dog
And called her Penny.
She was very small and quiet
And had her odd fears.
But that all changed over the years.
Now she is still small but proud.
And from being quiet,
She's very, very loud.
She enjoys going for walks
And chasing all the birds,
Whatever the weather
She never really cares.
She walks proudly
Down the street.
Sniffing at lamp-posts
Sniffing at feet.
She lifts her head up high
Looking tidy and neat.

Julia Tomlinson (13) Darwen Moorland High School

IN MY HEAD

In my head,
It's always telling me which lessons to go to next,
What homework I have today,
Oh and by the way,
Don't forget to revise for your test, it says.

My head tells me when to sit and stand,
It tells me to take my dog for a walk
And she talks me across the land
And when to be quiet and when to talk.

My head tells me lots of other things,
More than you can imagine,
My head is quite brainy
Is yours?

Joanne Louise Burrow (12) Darwen Moorland High School

A REAL THROW AWAY

I sit and think of the past,
The way it used to be,
When I had a family,
When the family had me.

I used to have a house,
I used to have a car,
I used to have a family,
But now it's tossed afar.

We went to a new place,
To find a new home,
But when we got there,
The job was gone.

We'd no money to move,
No jobs going,
We were broke
I'd even do mowing.

Our car broke down,
My family left,
I felt disheartened,
A real throw away.

I sit and think of the past,
The way it used to be,
When I had a family
When the family had me,
A real throw away.

Bernadette O'Brien (12) Darwen Moorland High School

LADS

You get them fat
You get them small
Some girls get loads
Some none at all.

They make you sad
They make you cry
Why do we have 'em
Girls wonder why.

They're a waste of space
A waste of flesh
They shouldn't be free
Should be kept behind mesh!

If lads are reading
Don't take offence
It's just a joke
So don't get tense.

Leanne Youd (13) Darwen Moorland High School

FOOTBALL

Pick up my boots and my shin-pads
Sunday afternoon off with the lads
Playing against a really good team
Scoring the winning goal, oh what a dream
There goes the whistle the ref starts the match
Let's hope their keeper just can't catch
It's now half-time, nil-nil is the score
I wish it was 2-0 to us or even more
One minute to go and I put one in
We've won the match and the crowd make a din.

Peter Monks (12) Fulwood High School

MY DOG PENNY

My dog Penny does nothing but chew,
She's got no brains, well, maybe a few.
Penny really isn't that dumb,
At least she eats tinned Pedigree Chum.

My dog Penny is really strong,
I can pull her, but not for long.
My dog Penny is growing fast,
When she's an adult, she'll be big at last.

My dog Penny is still quite small,
But when she's an adult she'll be quite tall.
We will all just have to cry,
When it is time to say goodbye.

Paul Anderton (11) Fulwood High School

MY FEELINGS

My feelings are trapped inside,
They must not show,
They must hide,
I feel low,
I feel blue,
There's nothing I can do.

My love has gone,
Gone is the sun,
I have no life,
It's all trouble and strife.

They ask what's wrong,
My life just can't go on,
I sit there just bored,
Please help me Lord.

Pinky Kaur (13) Fulwood High School

WAR

Steam rises from an empty gun barrel
And death engulfs the land
A cannon bellows its deafening sound
Corpses lie in a bed of sand.

Bullets slice through the night's heat
And the earth lets out a cry
Men stand ready for battle
Ready and willing to die.

A warplane flies with sonic speed
Above our armoured heads
Tonight the lights will shine again
Over the corpses of a sandy bed.

Buildings shatter upon the hill
As they move in to end the fight
Bullets strike my wasted body
And darkness vanishes the light.

My last breath tears from wounded lungs
And I know it must end like this
My limp body tenses to meet the end
My last thoughts of what I shall miss . . .

Chris Stevenson (14) Fulwood High School

MIDNIGHT

It is a full moon at 12 in the night,
The witches will fly and the werewolves will bite.
The zombies and the ghosts will be your hosts,
To the most gruesome show you've ever seen.
The stars of the show are strange monsters and beasts,
Eyeing each other as a slap-up feast.
They could rip off your head and kill you real quick,
It is so disgusting it'll make you feel sick.

Jamie Roskell (12) Fulwood High School

THE WEATHER

When I look out of the window
I just sit there and gaze
And wish that in the near future
The sun would shine for days.
But when I take a second look
I know it won't come true
Because now as winter is here
Rain is all it will do.

The only thing left to do
Is daydream to myself,
Of bright and colourful trees,
Little pixies and elves
But as I come back to life
I sit there in a mood
And think about other things
Such as netball and food.

Natalie Rees (14) Fulwood High School

THE SUPER NINTENDO

The Super Nintendo is in the lead,
Ahead of Sega's Megadrive machine.
With games like Mario, Fifa Football,
Makes no difference whether you're young or old.

Sports, fighting, shooting and platform games,
Going on other consoles isn't the same.
Different joypads, joysticks and add ons,
Many fighting games require combinations.

For some readers there's computer magazines,
With all these things and more, you should be keen.
To go down to the shops and buy a machine,
For eighty quid with Street Fighter it's a great deal.

Andrew Ashworth (13) Fulwood High School

CAKES

Cakes are delicious and scrummy,
They are light and fluffy in your tummy,
They make you feel nice inside,
But really they're doing no good,
The calories pile on every time.
So every time you have a cake,
Just remember these 3 little words,
Calories, calories, calories.

Emma Worrell (12) Fulwood High School

THE SOUND OF THE RAIN

It's wet again outside as I look,
The river overflows and so does the brook.
The sun doesn't appear as much anymore,
It's rain, rain, rain, oh it does get a bore!

I stare at the puddles that gather in clumps,
I wish I could be out there but I've come down with
The mumps.
Nobody cares that I'm stuck in my bed,
All this boredom really goes to my head.

That's why I sit here for most of the day,
Hoping this illness will soon go away.
My mum has gone to work,
My sister went off to school,
They've left me on my own to weep and drool.

I lie here on my own trying to get to sleep,
It gets so boring I really want to weep.
But at the end of the day in hurt or in pain,
I'll always hear the sound of the rain.

Julie Oldfield (13) Fulwood High School

GREENS

I do hate eating greens,
especially carrots and kidney beans.
Everyone says that they're good for you,
don't believe that, it's not true!
Cabbage, cauliflower and sprouts too,
no more please I think I'm going to s.w.
I do hate eating greens,
especially carrots and kidney beans.

Hitesh Tailor (12) Fulwood High School

THE DAY I WAS GROUNDED

When I was grounded once one day,
I found I couldn't go out to play.
I pleaded with my mum and dad,
But they just said, 'No, you've been bad.'
They sent me up into my room,
And all I felt was doom and gloom.
I looked out through my window pane.
And thought my parents were insane.
I planned to escape and run away,
And vowed to make my parents pay.
So I climbed out on the window sill,
But there was dad, ready to kill.
'Because you tried to run away,
Now you're grounded another day.'

Darren Jackson (12) Fulwood High School

SAVE IT

In the rainforests you will see
Poverty not harmony
Trees burning
Charcoal churning
This is what you now see
This is what the world is blaming on me

Causing damage every day
Causing damage in every way
Animals dying
Children crying
This is what you now see
This is what the world is blaming on me

Cut down trees on the ground
Burning trees all around
From children's toys
To villages destroyed
This is what you now see
This is what the world is blaming on me

Save it today and there's a glimmer of hope
Tomorrow it could be left hanging on a rope
Dying, poisoned by gold
People that are young and old
This is what you now see
This is what the world is blaming on me.

Vicky Pickles (12) Fulwood High School

WHAT I'M SCARED OF . . .

I'm scared of a tiger,
  escaping from the zoo.
I'm scared of my dog,
  being run over by you.
I'm scared of a dark
  and lonely street.
I'm scared of the monster,
  that's at my feet.
I'm scared of being drowned,
  by the whirling sea.
These are the things,
  that really scare me.

I'm scared of the snakes,
  that have a nasty bite.
I'm scared of getting into
  a great big fight.
I'm scared of getting hurt,
  from a crash in a car.
I'm scared of having an operation
  and getting a scar.
I'm scared of getting bitten,
  by hundreds of dogs.
I'm scared of getting thrown into a fire,
  with tons of logs.
I'm scared of being stung,
  by an enormous bee.
These are the things,
  that really scare me.

Beth Squire (12) Fulwood High School

DEATH BY HAMSTER

Across the carpet,
It spies its prey.
The hamster's out
Again today.

Death by Hamster,
As you should know,
Is not the nicest
Way to go.

He spots the target -
Someone's knee.
He'll kill the enemy,
Painfully.

He leaps up quickly,
Onto their shoe
And thinks to himself,
This is easy to do.

About to clamber
Up the leg.
Falls down, and off
And *squish!* He's dead.

And the moral of this story is:
Why have hamster repellent,
When you can have Doc Martens?

Daniel Huntley (13) Fulwood High School

EXCUSES

My friend got some chocolates,
I got some skin cream.
He said, 'You've got enough
Spots without me helping!'

My friend got some flowers,
I got a catalogue.
He said, 'The flowers in there
Don't need watering and last longer.'

My friend got some new shoes,
I got a pumice stone.
He said, 'It's uncomfortable
With corns on your feet.'

My friend got a framed picture,
I got a sketch pad.
He said, 'You can draw something
And frame it yourself.'

My friend got a silk heart,
I got an onion.
He said, 'Well you can't eat
A silk heart, can you?'

Erica Fowler (14) Garstang High School

THE BULLY

Why?
Why did I say nothing?
Why did I do nothing?
I should have said something
I chose to tolerate him
Big mistake
I was not scared
He could physically injure me
But his words
They are what hurt.
The constant taunting,
The vicious rumours and untrue tales.
I let him get away with it
Telling only my best friend.
My life began to be hell
And still I did nothing
Why?

Andrew Crook (14) Garstang High School

MEMORY OF YOU

It started so recently.
When you, my best friend,
Began to act differently.
From being so nice,
You changed,
Your clothes were more outlandish
Than mine,
You said I was boring.
I felt strange with you.
You began to experiment
With things I disapproved of.
You tried to make me be the same,
But I can't be like you.
Sorry,
I wanted us to be friends.
But you, you drove me away.
Can't you see it's *your* behaviour
That has alienated us?
Not mine?
I don't know you now,
Where did you go?
The person I once liked,
I wish we could go back in time,
Stay the same,
Forever friends.

Karen Cross (14) Garstang High School

APOLOGY FOR KATE

People used to say we were like two peas in a pod,
Kate and I.
We were like sisters.
Liked the same music, the same clothes -
like sisters.

I was so angry when my mother told me;
angry with Kate, with her parents, with myself.
Furious that she hadn't told me.

'A better education' was how her parents phrased it.
Better? Better for whom?
I was petrified of going to school -
to that lonely forlorn place.
Who would I sit with?
Who would I partner in games?
My mother droned on about making new friends.
She didn't understand the loss I felt.
I cried.

I saw her standing at the bus stop -
long brown skirt, blazer and briefcase.
Me in my old cardigan, kneesocks and backpack.
She was chatting to her friends, her new friends.
I felt ripped apart by jealousy and sadness.
I stood motionless by the roadside,
she looked up, smiled, beckoned to me,
but I lowered my head and walked on by.

I glanced back, you looked hurt
and for a moment I felt glad -
but now I'm sorry Kate. Who deserted whom?

Rachel Goldspink (14) Garstang High School

IF ONLY

She was my best friend
We'd known each other since . . .
We would sit together in class
We would eat together for dinner
We would read the same books.

At playtime we'd run around
Like squirrels jumping and skipping.

Then the day of the accident.
After school we would walk
Home together.
That day we didn't, she was going
To town with her mum.

I saw her, outside the school gates.
She was crossing the road when
A car came out of nowhere
Racing up the road.
She didn't see it in time . . .

She was taken away in an
Ambulance, unconscious.
I just stood there, saying nothing.
I kept thinking if only . . .
If only I had been there . . . If only . . .

She died before she got
To the hospital.
I turned into a very
Quiet girl after the accident.
I wouldn't, I couldn't
Understand why? Why?
I will never forget you . . .
Louise.
x

Laura Newton (14) Garstang High School

A FRIEND?

I never knew when he was a friend,
None of the others were like him,
I never knew if he was speaking the truth,
No-one did,
He constantly lied to everyone,
His whole life was a lie,
One big charade,
One big act to impress everyone,
But no-one was impressed,
They all knew what he was like,
I should have seen earlier,
He used me,
He used me to play my drums,
He used me to get to my friends,
But they knew,
They saw what he was like from the start,
It's his fault,
He shouldn't have lied,
He should have given up his childish ways,
He should have shown more adult demeanour,
If he didn't want to turn out the way he did.

David Parker (14) Garstang High School

84

WHAT HAVE I DONE?

The alarm rings at seven o'clock, Monday, another week at school,
I get washed, dressed, slowly of course,
What's the point of rushing?
I come downstairs, it's half past seven,
Half an hour before I see them.
Another week of their taunting,
Their snide remarks and their faces.
It's not fair, why me?
What have I done?
The clock says eight o'clock, got to get going.
Mum gives me a supportive look before I turn the corner.
A short walk before I see them.
Maybe I can break my leg and be off school for a while.
Maybe an illness where I don't have to come to school.

I didn't break my leg
Or get an illness.
I lived through it.
The anger, the pain,
It's all gone now,
But the regret of what I didn't do and should have done is as strong
As the memory.

Victoria Speedwell (14) Garstang High School

TOO LATE

I wish I could have said goodbye,
To my uncle John that is.
I can't remember what he looked like,
But I remember visiting his house,
I can't even remember where he lived,
But I wish that I could.
All that I have left is his pen,
And probably some old photos.
I can remember my dad's stories
About him sinking in the war,
And I can remember the five pounds,
Every birthday, every Christmas, never late.
I can remember wanting to visit him,
But now, it's too late, much too late.

Alex Sharp (14) Garstang High School

POP

Pressure is
forced right up
to the top.
When the cork is released
the pressure will pop.
Froth will rise up,
crawl out of the neck,
then bubble down slowly
all over the deck.

Tip the bottle sideways
right into the glass.
It soon overflows and
causes a splash.
Pick the glass up as it
sparkles away.
Sit and be merry
and drink all the day.

Nicola Guyer (13) Gawthorpe High School

MONDAY MORNING

On Monday morning I get up,
'Oh no it's school,' I say,
I pour some orange in my cup,
And get ready for the day.

I get to school at half past nine,
Although we start at eight,
My best friend says I'll get a fine,
Because I have been late.

I get told that I've been very bad,
And I haven't to do it again,
This makes me feel very mad,
So I blame it all on Ben.

Ben gets his gang to jump on me,
I get a big black eye,
They squash me like a little pea,
Why? Oh why? Oh why?

When I get home,
My mother says,
'What has happened to you?'
Then she leaves me all alone,
Because she's gone to a do!

She'll come home around half past ten,
No doubt she'll go straight to bed,
So I'll be able to watch tele till then,
And then I'll snuggle up wi' mi' ted.

Rebecca Greenwood (14) Gawthorpe High School

HALLOWE'EN

Hallowe'en is coming near,
Don't be afraid it's nothing to fear.
The witches will have you in stitches,
The wizards will make a big blizzard.
The witches and wizards all come together,
But don't get too attached they are not here forever.
Let's all have a game of apple bobbing,
It's too much noise, my head is throbbing.
Hallowe'en is coming near,
Don't be afraid it's nothing to fear.

Farzana Gul (12) Haslingden High School

SOUTH AFRICA

Look at the shanty towns
All those hungry people
Babies in dirty ragged gowns
Life for the blacks is most unfair
Whites always have the biggest share
With black children fighting for their way of life
South Africa's struggle is one of strife.

John Breeze (12) Haslingden High School

GOING SHOPPING

It's all in the car,
We're not going far.
It's only a short hop,
We're going for the weekly shop.
Everybody out,
There's no need to shout.
Go and fetch a trolley,
And hurry up about it Molly!
Up and down each aisle,
All in single file.
Dad's getting in a mood,
Do we need all this food?
The trolley has had its fill,
Now off we go to the till.
How much did you say?
I suppose I'd better pay.
Loading up the boot,
What a load of loot.
Dad's starting to moan,
The car is starting to groan,
Along the bumpy road,
Off we go with our heavy load.
Now we've got back,
It's time to unpack.
Put the food away,
Ready for another day.
Only a week to go,
And what do you know?
It's all in the car,
We're not going far.

Lucy Deaville (11)   Hathershaw School

THE GOLDEN RIVER

The sky was sharp as needles,
The day was bright as snow,
The river that I found had a lovely golden glow.
When all of a sudden it started,
The thunderous sky opened and the electric waves parted.
Two horns poked out of the water,
He looked like he was out to slaughter.
His eyes came next and then his fangs,
His fork and then his hands.
Then if by magic it faded away,
The sky all cleared up
And again it was a beautiful day.

Carly Urquhart (12) Highfield High School

THE TEACHER'S PESTS

'Get down boy don't be a pest,
You silly fool, I'm not impressed.
Now get writing or you'll miss your break,
You silly boy, hurry up, for God's sake!'

'Sorry Sir, I forgot my book.'
'Thomas Sniper, you little crook,
I might have known you would forget,
But I've not finished with you yet!

Now come along, don't sit around,
Do your work and don't make a sound.
I'm really fed up with this stupid class,
All they do is fight and harass.

The break bell's gone, oh what a shame,
But your excuses are so lame.
So I'm not going to let you go,
If it takes today or tomorrow.

I'll keep you in until it's done,
Is that clear, Rebecca Lunn!
And I don't care what your parents say,
As far as I'm concerned it's okay.

Now we'll do Maths to finish the day,
What's five times five, Oliver Tay?'
'Is it twenty-seven? I'm sure it is right.'
'You stupid boy, get out of my sight!

Don't you know a simple sum,
God blimey boy, you're so dumb!
Ah yes, the 3.30 bell has gone,
And today, I admit, has been very long.

So I am going to let you go, just today,
But tomorrow, oh boy, there'll be hell to pay!'

Lukvinder Kaur (13) Kersal High School

THE TRAIN

People climb in, looking for a seat,
A hundred people, two hundred feet.
The train starts up, the passengers jerk back,
Everyone listening to the clickety clack.

The train picks up speed, rushing ahead,
It's entering London, so the driver said.
It gradually slows down, the squeak of the brakes,
Then comes to a halt with a shuddering shake.

The train starts up, after the rest,
Heading towards the sunset in the far west.
The trees' leaves rustle as the train rushes past,
It sounds its horn and carries on fast.

It finally stops at the last station of the day,
People get off and go on their way.
The train shuts off, the engine dies down,
Everything is still . . . not a solitary sound.

Claire Hyde (14) Kersal High School

THE CHRISTMAS RUSH

From shop to shop,
The people scurry,
Longing to be in their warm houses.

But in the rain,
They do not see,
The child hiding,
Like a frightened mouse.

Hoping someone
Will take pity,
And give him the food
He so much needs.

They just ignore him
Saying, 'I don't care,'
Wishing he would go away,
Advice to feed him they do not heed.

Sat by the fire,
Not unlike their cats,
They forget what they saw today,
As they rest their heads.

But the little boy
Goes to sleep
And does not wake up,
They don't care that he is dead.

Daniel Norris (13) Kersal High School

THE EMPTY HOUSE

As I look out of my window
I see it standing there
With all its broken windows
It looks so very bare.
They've boarded up its windows
Wind still blows in and out
It's haunted all our street says
But I still have my doubts.

As I walked past the old garden
A girl was standing there
As if she couldn't speak
Just listen, stand and stare.
She pointed to the empty house
As if to say it's mine
She stared at me for quite a while
She looked so meek and kind
Inside I bet it's really cold
The frost lying all about
It's haunted all our street says
But I still have my doubts.

They say there's a vote to pull it down
I really think they shouldn't
If I was old enough to vote
I wouldn't let them, I wouldn't.
They say to fix all the damages
It would cost an enormous amount
All our street say it's haunted
But I still have my doubts.

Rachael Hunter (13) Kersal High School

THE PERFECT WORLD

The roads are clean, another perfect day,
No-one crying or hurt, everyone is happy

Just another day in the perfect world.

The houses are proper and prim,
All with white picket fences,
All smiles and laughing,
Children playing

Just another day in the perfect world.

The happiness suddenly fades away,
The night comes out, disappears the day,
The gangs come round, it's time to *play*,
Not really the very perfect way

Just another day in the perfect world.

They hound you and chase you until you fall, running, running
                                        not noticing the wall.
Crunch, you've collided, now you're done for, they hit you
                              and hurt you, they make you sore.
Night turns to day, day turns to night once again, another fight.
A stone is thrown, a brick is hurled, not the very perfect world.
The perfect hour, the perfect minute, 60 seconds of hell are in it.
You've been chased, hurt, caught by the neck, you look around,
                                        not very perfect.
You look back at the *perfect world* you left, lying, slowly dying,
                              staring at death . . .

David W Jones (13) Kersal High School

96

CATS AND DOGS IN WINTER

Cats and dogs roam the streets,
looking for a place to sleep.
They turn a corner, what will they see?
Just another dirty back street.
All the children are in their homes,
while the animals are out alone.

The nights are dark, the stars are out.
Is that all the people care about?
They head towards the dark black alley,
which is really smelly.

The cats and dogs all stand still,
frozen in the midnight chill.
The dark, black clouds fade away.
Here is another rainy day.
The thunder and lightning scares them all.
They wish they were all indoors.

They sit outside their owner's doors,
with their damp, wet and muddy paws.
Then one day they would succeed.
Their owners would let them in to
have some food.

Emma Wilkinson (13) Kersal High School

VIOLENCE

A group of boys walking down the street,
The clothes they're wearing, the shoes upon their feet,
All the new fashion, all the new code,
Walking proudly down the road.

Nobody knows what's in their heads,
The thought of fear and the dead.
This group may have something to hide,
Deep, deep down amongst their pride.

A little old woman walking to the phone,
A little afraid and all alone.
A tap on the window startles her,
The shudder of fear goes through her.

The metal bar clashes,
The window smashes,
One quick hit towards the head,
Knocks her down, but is she dead?

Suddenly the car comes to a halt,
Whilst the young boy undoes the bolt,
Into the house they quickly creep,
Not even bothering to wipe their feet.

The sound of guns, screams and squeals,
So much amount of pain we feel.
Why can't we just have silence?
Instead we have to resort to violence.

Sarah Liza Barrow (13) Kersal High School

SALFORD

Crash! A car goes zooming by,
Not driven by the owner, it's stolen that's why.
The 'go for a spin' on a football pitch,
Then burn the car out in a ditch.
There's joyriding everywhere in Salford.

The engine screams, the wheels spin,
Smash through the window, then they're in.
Then out they get and fill up the boot.
Everything in the shop is 'loot'.
There's ramraiding everywhere in Salford.

Don't walk the streets at night, alone;
It's much safer in your home:
'Give us your trainers,' the big one said,
Then a baseball bat meets with your head.
There's gang violence everywhere in Salford.

Smash the glass, through the window,
Everywhere's locked; they still get in though.
Grab the telly, then the computer,
Break anything that's glass or pewter.
There's breaking and entering everywhere in Salford.

'Where's my money? You owe me big; what's more
don't squeal to no pig!'
No answer; the dealer pulls a gun, his frightened
'customer' starts to run;
One shot goes off, a laugh with glee,
He hit his target in the knee.
There's drug-related violence everywhere in Salford.

Salford isn't really that bad;
Just full of people who're mad,
OK, so the crime is high, it's where I live.
Maybe where I'll die.
I like it everywhere in Salford.

James Creely (14) Kersal High School

SECRETS

I've got some secrets, no-one must know,
I must be careful to not let them show,
Secrets are private and hidden away,
No-one will find them, I'm glad to say.

Everyone has secrets to keep,
Most are good, some are bad,
Some you wish you never had,
I like the secrets that give surprises.

I kept a secret on Mother's Day,
I took her her breakfast in bed on a tray;
Bought her a necklace
And hid it away -

How much I paid,
I will not say,
Or else my secret would be
Out and away.

David M Cole (13) Lancaster Royal Grammar School

QUESTION

A world without life,
Is like a tree without leaves.
It does not breathe,
It does not eat.
Worst of all, it does not grow.

So why might you ask,
Do we all destroy it?
'Cause all the biologists know,
Without the trees, we cannot breathe
And without the sun and rain,
No-one will reign,
The land filled with food.
With all the gases
We put into the air,
You have to think,
'What about my sunblock?'
If I forget to put it on,
Will I be a piece of fried bacon?

Maybe we stop,
And think about the world,
So generations can come
Out of the unborn dimension.

Helen Audsley (15) Lytham St Anne's High School

SOME BUT NOT ALL

Politicians are an
Artificial
Form of intelligence
Nothing they ever do ever makes any sense
Greed, ego
And emotional blindness
Turns souls into robotic
Chaos and mess
Their ears tightly closed to the voices of the land
Yet they hold your whole life
In the palms of their hands
What chance does peace have
With politicians who gamble?
A classless society is really a shambles
Morals form the gutter
Always watching their backs
Ex mistresses pose
For the newspaper hacks
Citizen's rights, an unwritten constitution
Repeatedly ignored
Will result in revolution
Incessant handshaking
Ingratiating smiles
Big brother is watching, you're kept on their files
They keep workers' wages down
At *acceptable* levels
Pensioners freeze
Whilst politicians toast, next the fires of hell
Discriminating quotas
Where are the women?
Ancient ways of thinking
Men think themselves the shaman
There are lies
White lies

Damned lies and statistics
There are Liberals
Tories
Labour and all politics.

Hanan Souaidi (14) Lytham St Anne's High School

JUST ANOTHER BROKEN FAMILY

She stares at the walls
of the pit she calls home,
The baby is screaming,
she's all alone.

She turns up the TV
to drown out the noise,
She thinks of his past life
her friends and the boys.

She's just got the Giro
it's smaller each week,
It's hardly enough for
the baby to eat.

Her plight gets more desperate
as the weeks go by,
She is so stricken she
just wants to die.

This is her life
not a penny to her name,
She thinks it's her fault but
the government's to blame.

Jeff Gaskell & Christian Elliott (15)
Lytham St Anne's High School

DETACHED

Black mob of mixed writers,
Gazing, staring, wondering,
At trainers on walls,
Their thud on the floor
Next door.
Clattering of objects,
Voices shouting,
Shriek whistle cutting through.
The cold of a door
Heavy against my foot
Pressing, shutting out.
Then leaving the dark behind
For light outside.
A giggle from girls
Chattering past.
The roar of machines louder -
New orange brickwork
Against old orange leaves,
Whispering.
Balls bounce, propelled
By runners.
Masks watching
Over *no entry,* staring.
Turn ninety degrees and
Voice now in stereo,
Surrounding the silent booth.
Light struggles through
Mottled glass above,
The corridor the *rotastak* -
Ourselves the hamsters.
Ponderous footsteps crescendo
In authority,
A rush of air,
Squeal of dry hinges . . .
Bang.

Helen Smith (15) Lytham St Anne's High School

104

SHEEP

Independence starts at the moment of propagation,
from then life is a battle raging,
raging between moments of redemption.

For you the map is read, the road chosen,
before your first gasp of air
your future is charted.

Streets and alleys become dead ends
and the fast moving road of life becomes
a tunnel with no escape, no turning back.

Personality, a mere deviation on the conformities,
suggested and demanded by the powers that be.
Conform, become mature and responsible.

I tried to grasp responsibility but slipped.
Emancipate yourself from mental slavery,
none but yourself can free your mind.

And when the baying pack cries out
for you to follow the tunnel,
Remember, life is what you make it.

James Palmer (16) Lytham St Anne's High School

LIFE AND THE WORLD

Punish me as you will,
I do no wrong,
You walked on me,
Though I remained so strong,

I gave you your life,
You waste it with death,
Without me you're nothing,
No more than a breath,

My soils are rich,
My skies so fine,
Your wars tore this up,
It's no longer mine,

Nuclear weapons tear my skin,
Bombs rip my hide,
Stop this destruction,
You have no pride,

The life I give,
So meaninglessly lost,
Now I care not,
You shall pay the cost.

Adam Mercer (13) Lytham St Anne's High School

CHANGE

She tears up the piece of paper,
looking at it with a frown.
Yet another job lost,
It's really getting her down.

She piles in with the shopping,
her man shouts, 'Where's my tea?'
The kids run up, she sighs,
wishing she was free.

For her children things are changing,
for better not for worse.
Now they can look for different jobs,
Not teacher, cook, or nurse.

She scours the local papers,
nothing yet again.
Trying to better herself? What's the point,
when the world's full of men.

Kathryn Moore (15) Lytham St Anne's High School

A CALL FOR HELP

In my room there is a window,
Outside I want to be.
My world's within four walls,
Yours is wide and free.

You may think I'm a prisoner,
Well I am of such a kind.
But you see I am not guilty,
I'm innocent and blind.

Laura Mallinson (15) Lytham St Anne's High School

HUMPTY DUMPTY

Humpty Dumpty sat on the wall,
Humpty Dumpty had a great fall,
Off he was rushed to a hospital nearby,
'We have no beds, give another a try.'
They travelled far to find a bed.
Before they got there poor Humpty was dead.

People keep on dying,
But the government aren't trying.
The NHS need money,
Situations like this aren't funny.

Natalie Wood (14) Lytham St Anne's High School

THOUGHTS OF THE HOMELESS

Open your eyes
And you will see,
The difference between
You and me.

There you are
Well-clothed and well-fed.
Where all I have
Is the street, for a bed.

My only things
Are what you give to me,
When your conscience is pricked
By the squalor you see.

All the things I possess
Are given by you,
Just think!
You could be me, too.

Hilary Stuart (15) Lytham St Anne's High School

LIFE IS A SERIES OF CHOICES

Life is a series of choices,
Or so the saying goes,
Which path will I choose to follow,
The answer nobody knows.

It's not a dress rehearsal,
You've only got one shot,
The scene is ever changing,
An ever moving plot.

Exams dominate my thoughts,
What grades will I achieve?
It's going to really matter,
On the day we take our leave.

A job, a course, maybe a degree,
It's not easy to decide,
But one thing is for certain,
From this I cannot hide.

But doubts are gathering in my mind,
Just take a look around
Millions of people on the dole,
With no jobs to be found.

It can be so depressing,
Will I be on my own?
Will I find a partner?
Will I have a home?

They say life slips by quickly,
And soon I will be old,
And all the choices have been made,
And my story has been told.

Life is a series of choices,
Or so the saying goes,
Let's just take one step at a time,
My poem now I close.

Kate Rogan (16) Lytham St Anne's High School

THE HUMAN RACE

Aerosols full of CFC's,
Is this how our world should be?
There are no dolphins in the sea,
The next generation will have to pay the fee.

Unleaded petrol is the way to go,
Or else our world will be a poor show.
Fur coats should be a thing of the past,
Or else our animals will not last.

Trees are lying on the ground,
All piled up in a great big mound.
Recycled paper's what we need,
To satisfy man's massive need!

So if you're clever and have listened
To what we've just truthfully written.
The world will be a better place,
For all the entire human race.

Vicky Haslingden & Amy McDonald (12)
Lytham St Anne's High School

OUTSIDE THE WINDOW

We sit together. Alone.
We talk, we discuss, scream unheard,
listen intently, listen to the cars,
the people, the life we see and
hear of on the telly,
in the news . . .
outside the window

We learn together. Alone.
We laugh, we cry, we learn,
we dream, dream of the life
we see and hear of on the telly,
in the news . . .
outside the window.

We progress together. Alone.
We hate, we love, we plead,
we run, run from the life
we see and hear of on the telly,
in the news . . .
outside the window

We stand together. Alone.
We face, we turn, we fight,
we fear, fear the life
we see and hear of on the telly,
in the news . . .
outside the window

We fall together. Alone.
We laugh, we cry, we hate, we love.
We dream.

Victoria Hornby (16) Lytham St Anne's High School

THE ASYLUM

Pushed out onto chequered tiles that echo,
Furtive footsteps as we move slowly down,
Or up? The corridor, subdued green adorns the cold,
empty, diagram strewn walls.
Yrtne On read the reverse signs on the transparent double doors
Scoretwonilreds blares from somewhere else
and bounces off the walls
like a hollow leather ball
Three figures pass, puzzled at our still, statuesque stances
Then continue on their bewildered way left to ponder at our intentions
Moving on, a yellow monster tears mercilessly away,
at the wounded earth, flinging chunks high into the air
A gust of cooling air brushes my face, an airy, dry cobweb.
Pale blue sky looks weak and shallow like a puddle
Inside all is death cold, more a morgue for the living than a school
Zombie students move like puppets on tramlines,
Down those graveyard morbid corridors
Of chequered tiles,
More chequered tiles,
And more,
Orange bin.

Tom Wigham (15) Lytham St Anne's High School

WAR
Trench warfare from the viewpoint of a soldier

It was cold, it was damp, there was mud all around,
I could see my friends dying, I could see bodies in the ground,
The order came to go over the top,
I heard the machine gun, saw men stop,
Dead, dying, everywhere,
And none of the Generals really could care,
Another body falls covered in blood,
The only coffin he'll get is a coffin of *mud.*
Kitcherner said, 'Britain needs *you*,'
But it won't make any difference he'll only kill you off too.
You're too young, but you signed up anyway,
But you won't live long enough to collect your first pay!
A whole generation killed off just like that,
And on your son's body the rats are getting fat.
Rats, rats everywhere,
Rats, rats they seem to cluster there,
Another one dies, the rats are there quick,
To eat up the body, I hate it, it's sick.
Rats, rats they're at your food.
The conditions we live in really are crude,
Four walls of mud, and a cesspit for the floor,
There's only one way out, there's only one door,
Over the top, attack enemy lines,
Get shot to pieces, step on some mines,
If you survive there's barbed wire too,
You've got no bullets, your time's up, you're through!
You fall off your feet, you die in the mud,
You are a failure. You didn't make it. No good.

Tim Cox (14) Montgomery High School

THE DYING WORLD

It was peaceful,
A beautiful sight.
The day was turning,
Turning into night.

The heartfelt sun set
Reached out to the heart,
Before it was gone,
Gone to depart.

The hour was sweet,
Sweet and clear.
But not for long
You must consider.

That the world is dying
Dying in grace
A terrible loss
To the human race.

Yet if they were here
Here in the countryside
They would think,
Think to decide

Philip Blackwell (14) Montgomery High School

AUTUMN

As the days are getting long
and the leaves are on the ground
you can tell that winter is near.

Kimberly Hall (11) Our Lady's High School, Preston

SINCE I WAS A LAD

I'm an old man, and I remember the war,
I remember all the football matches, even the score.
No televisions, and that's no lie,
If you wanted entertainment, you'd have to watch paint dry.
At the age of ninety nine, I'm not doing so bad,
But everything has changed, since I was a lad.

No 'ealthy drinks, like 'erbal tea,
'cos a proper cup o' tea would satisfy me.
None of these toys that power off 'lectric,
None of these lengths that measure in metric.
At the ripe old age, that I am, you'd think that I was mad,
But everything has changed, you see, since I was a lad.

None of these shoes, with air in the sole,
In my day the shoes were made out of coal.

Things today aren't quite the same,
Things are more arranged.
Yet even though we have moved on,
The weather hasn't changed.

Noel Billington (12) Our Lady's High School, Preston

THE HOLE OF DEATH

The dark deep tunnel of water,
Pouring into the hole of death,
A man falling to his doom,
The grave stones he imagined,
Abandoned and neglected,
The end is drawing near,
For soon he'll be there.

Catherine Hughes (12) Our Lady's High School, Preston

MY GHOST POEM

One night I could not get to sleep,
And so I started counting sheep,
I got up to fifty four,
Then I heard the creaking door.

I told myself it's in my head,
And snuggled up in my bed,
It started creeping up the stairs,
And I began to say my prayers.

My door opened and in the light,
I saw a ghost shining bright,
It walked across my bedroom floor,
Then disappeared through an invisible door.

Lisa Gornall (12) Our Lady's High School, Preston

CHRISTMAS SHOPPING

Christmas shopping, what a drag,
Far behind my dad, I lag,
Please help me, where are the loos?
My feet are rubbing in my shoes.

My arms twice as large from my bags,
Gift wrap boxes and gift tags,
We stop off for a very quick drink,
With my legs on the brink.

I get home, at last I can rest,
But I forgot a gift for my sister the pest.

Caroline Quinn (12) Our Lady's High School, Preston

116

ROLLERCOASTERS

Up and down,
round and round,
they'll turn your tummy,
upside down
they'll make you sick,
they'll make you scream,
they'll make you want to,
go again.

Lynsey Turner (13) Our Lady's High School, Preston

CORONATION STREET!

Come on everybody let's stamp your feet
We're going down to Coronation Street.
There's Curly Watts with the spiky hair
And bossy Vera is always there,

Now Mavis Wilton she's a twit
And Jack he's fat you gotta admit.
Bet Gilroy stands behind the bar
Serving Mike Baldwin with the fancy car.

There's Derek Wilton the weird salesman
He can't sell a thing but he's Mavis' man.
Now Betty makes all the grub
She serves it hot down at the pub.

Charlie drives the truck full of beer
It's a massive one to steer.
We all give a great big sigh
'Cause now it's time to say . . .
Goodbye!

Justine Machin (12) Our Lady's High School, Preston

NIGHTMARE

I am walking through the forest
The moon is in the sky.
The trees are all around me.
I think I am going to die.
I hear footsteps behind me.
My heart is beating fast,
I am going round in circles
Not knowing if I will last.

Jenny Clegg (12) Our Lady's High School, Preston

TYPES OF GHOSTS!

There are ghosts which are happy,
Ghosts which are sad,
Ghosts that are jolly,
Ghosts that are mad,

There's ghosts that haunt,
Ghosts that can't see,
Some walk through walls
Or perhaps - you and me,

Ghosts that make noises,
Ghosts who can scare,
Or very nice ghosts,
But these are quite rare,

Some ghosts can kill you,
There are many types of ghosts,
Which ghost do *you* think,
You would like most?

Joanne Haggis (12) Our Lady's High School, Preston

CHRISTMAS EVE

It is Christmas Eve
And all is tense,
The magic of Christmas
Is about to begin,
The mince pies are cooking,
The smell is sweet,
The Christmas tree lights
Are glowing so bright,
Oh what will happen on
This Christmas night.

The stockings are hung
Upon the shelf,
And the sherry and pie
Are there as well,
The fire is burning,
The light shines bright,
It's getting late and
Time for bed,
Oh how I love Xmas.

Kate Loughran (13) Our Lady's High School, Preston

AUTUMN

Autumn is the time when leaves go brown,
And, when the wind blows, they all fall down.
The tree looks bare,
And I stand and stare
At all the dead leaves on the ground.

Christopher T Bowker (11) Our Lady's High School, Preston

MISCHIEF POEM

Mischief what does it mean to you?
To me it means a trick or two.
A pull of the chair,
A slap on the back
Could be enough for a heart attack.
Look at me, who am I?
I could deceive your untrained eye,
Mischief is what I do,
A hit from me,
A fall from you
And now I have to end this rhyme,
Because I'm running out of time
There is a victim over there,
I have to go and pull their hair.

Shelley Hull (13) Our Lady's High School, Preston

AN ODE TO SCHOOL!

Homework can be such a drag, if I don't do it teachers nag
In maths those numbers seem to swim,
and that's when I feel quite dim.
In English my spelling is really OK,
but speaking out loudly is when I stray away.
Now for history and all those dates, what a time it seems to take
Next is geography what a chore, all those maps can be a bore.
Art and design can take quite some time,
to turn thoughts into drawings and words into rhyme.
And now to sign off with my subjects galore,
I'll just say goodnight 'cos Roseanne's on 4!

Emma Williams (12) Our Lady's High School, Preston

120

THE FOX

The fox gently lowered his nose,
Tiptoeing about on his toes,
His thirsty mouth began to drink,
His feet in the mud began to sink.
His ears suddenly stood up tall,
He listens now with all his soul,
Yes, he hears again the foot of man,
So he picks himself up and runs as fast as
He can.
Now here comes the chase, they run so fast,
He wonders how long he will last.
Round the corner and under the gate,
Here comes the shot, his life they'll take,
Down goes the fox there's no way out,
The fox's confidence has turned to doubt,
Now he will die, 'cause he can't get up,
The fox's life the hunters took.

Elizabeth Anne Smith (11) Our Lady's High School, Preston

SEASONS

In summer it's hot, hot and warm
We laze on the beach till the summer storm
In autumn the leaves fall down, down down
Covering the pavements all over the town.
In winter it's cold, cold with bald trees
Frost covers the ground and we freeze.
In spring the new born life appears
Bringing warmth and calming our fears.

Gregory Winders (11) Our Lady's High School, Preston

SAM THE DOG

With a little round face,
      And gleaming eyes,
She pounds towards you,
      Wagging tail and all.

With a fierce bark,
      But a gentle growl,
She springs up and down,
      Like a bouncing ball.

So small and lively,
      With a glossy coat,
With trusting eyes,
      That say welcome home.

Jennifer L Gardner (12) Our Lady's High School, Preston

MY LITTLE SISTER

Her curly hair,
Her cheesy grin,
Her gleaming eyes that I look in.
The mischievous things she does to me,
Like hiding things and tickling me,
I know she doesn't mean no harm,
But it is hard to keep so calm.
Although my sister is a pain,
I still love her all the same.

Amy Wright (12) Our Lady's High School, Preston

ME DREAMING

I was sitting in my seat half asleep
fiddling with my pen wondering when . . .
all of a sudden Miss walks in
with a big fat grin under her chin.
Stop what you're doing sit up straight
listen to the bell *stop wait!*
The Queen's here today
tidy up yourself look where you're going . . .
Way hay!
Laura, Laura, are you here?
wake up you've been dreaming in class!
Laura wake up!

Laura Wilkinson (12) Our Lady's High School, Preston

SNOWFLAKE BABIES

Snowflake babies dropping to the ground,
So silent without a single sound,
Gently fading the star shaped lady,
Dancing like a Christian baby.
The moonlight reflection upon the surface,
Makes it shine with so much grace,
So when the snowflake lands upon it,
It makes the place look like dainty lace.
For this is the time for joy and happiness,
It makes you think of more, not less.
So when you're sat around your tree,
Think of the snowflake babies,
Who are fast asleep.

Lucia Cornacchione (13) Our Lady's High School, Preston

CHRISTMAS TIME

Christmas is a time for joy,
With lots of treats for girl and boy.
Teddies, dolls, bikes and cars,
Even yummy chocolate bars.

Presents wrapped in fancy paper
Only to be opened by children later.
Mothers make a Christmas dinner.
While children play a game called
Beat the winner.

Donna Louise Marie Massey (11) Our Lady's High School,
Preston

SEASONS

Spring is light and crisp,
The air is sharp and cool,
The trees sway in the breeze,
While the dew gathers in pools.

Summer is hot and dry,
The rain showers are often few,
The clouds are light and high,
And the sky is always blue.

Autumn is wet and windy,
The trees are red and gold,
The animals go to sleep,
While the children stand in the cold.

Winter is cold and jolly,
While people do Christmas shopping,
Everybody waits anxiously,
Until Christmas crackers are popping.

Jane L Eydmann (11) Our Lady's High School, Preston

MY PET GERBIL

I have a pet gerbil called Thumper,
who gets up in the middle of the night.
When I get up for a midnight feast he squeaks
and gives me a fright.
He nibbles my fingers and chews his cage,
'til I am in despair.
I got to the point where I was mad,
I simply couldn't care.
So I bought a cage and put him in,
he chewed that too - I just can't win!

Andrew Hunter (11) Our Lady's High School, Preston

SUMMER

The clocks go forward
The days are longer
Is summer really here?
The sun is shining
Everyone's smiling
Let's get out our holiday gear.

The warm wind's blowing
Grass is growing
Harvest time begins
The school is out
The children shout,
'Summer time is here!'
We rush to the coast
With our luggage and boats
For the happiest time of the year.

Joseph O'Malley (11) Our Lady's High School, Preston

BONFIRE NIGHT

The Roman torch,
It shines so bright,
It sometimes hides,
The night dark light.
Rockets flying everywhere,
Sparkling here,
Banging there.
Catherine wheels,
Whirring high,
Goodbye, goodbye,
They fade away,
And die.

Amanda Jackson (12) Our Lady's High School, Preston

THE LOCH NESS MONSTER

All was quiet on Loch Ness till,
Storm clouds began to gather,
The sky went from dim to dark.
The water began to stir,
The Loch Ness Monster began to whir.
he came out of the lake,
Crashed against the shore,
He then began to roar.
But he never got chance to finish,
Because the sun began to wake
As the storm began to break.

Michael Ainsworth (12) Our Lady's High School, Preston

THOUGHTS

There are days
I'm tired of being me,
The days I can't face reality.
The days will pass
That you went from me.
My life on earth seems eternity,
But life goes on in endless song
With all its trouble and its strife.
Is it a wonder I hate my life?
Do you still think of me?
Am I etched in your memory?
For so great a treasure
Words will never do.
I owe it to you
To see things through.
Surely promises are mine to give,
Because for our child I shall live.

Dawn Austin (15) Our Lady's High School, Preston

A WITCH'S SPELL!

Deer's eyes and a mouse's thighs.
Rabbit's brain, and a bat in pain.
A child's toe, a head of a doe.
Dinosaur's dinner, that's been squashed by a pillar.
Woodlice's spit and a human's zit.
A strangled pheasant, that doesn't look pleasant.
A slug's slimy trail and the shell of a snail.
Sleep from the eye and a vomit pie.
A hippopotamus tail, that won't fail!

Zoë Chadwick (12) Our Lady's High School, Preston

DRUGS

Try it once,
It won't harm me,
Try it twice,
I feel barmy,
Third time maybe I'm an addict,
Then I really start to panic.

Taking drugs has made me ill,
It all started when I took a pill,
Was it when I met that bloke,
Here he said, 'Try some Coke,'

I don't really want to die,
Now I wonder why?
Drugs don't only make you ill,
Taking drugs can make you *kill*,
Not just strangers you and me,
But also friends and family,

Best friends gone and all departed,
Mum and Dad broken hearted,
Can't remember how it started

Say *No* to drugs.

Natalie Dignan (14) Our Lady's High School, Preston

THE STARS ARE ALONE

Stars sit high in the sky,
They twinkle so bright at night,
So high in all their delight.

I wish I could join the stars,
Sleeping in the day,
The only things awake at night.

Alone with the moon,
But not alone,
Thousands of stars fly around together.

But yet still alone,
All alone, so alone,
All so far apart on their own.

I stop with a start as I realise,
The life of a star is no life for me,
As I would miss my friends and family.

Oh! I feel sorry for the stars,
The lonely stars,
I hope one day they won't be alone,
But together in perfect harmony.

Rachel Kelly (13) Our Lady's High School, Preston

NEVER FREE AGAIN - THE DOLPHIN'S STORY

As I swim free and easy,
Not a single care,
With my friends alongside me,
We are just not aware,
Of the dangers that are there.
Ready and waiting,
Those humans, those thieves,
That are chasing and chasing,
Poised to capture,
With their cruel snare.
We realise what is happening,
But now we are too late,
They want to take our freedom,
We are overwhelmed with fright,
Never free again.
As the net closes around me,
They do not understand,
But our anguish is silent,
We are trapped, no escape
                    Never free again.

Katharine Lonsdale (13) Our Lady's High School, Preston

MY TRAIN JOURNEY

Intercity,
Into the city,
Through the town,
Over a road,
Through some fields,
Then back into the city.

Intercity,
Into the city,
Stop at a station,
On come some people,
A whistle blows,
Then out of the city.

Intercity,
Out of the city,
Go past some houses,
Now past a golf course,
Next is my stop,
Now into my city.

Intercity,
Into the city,
Get all my luggage,
Go to the door, now,
The train stops,
I'm in the city.

Thomas Nolan (12) Our Lady's High School, Preston

NIGHTMARE

Life was normal and everything was fine,
It was early in the day around half past nine.
Nobody suspected what would happen . . . and then,
The bomb was dropped . . . it must of killed a thousand men.
When it happened luckily I was underground,
So the bomb did not harm me I was safe and sound.
When I came back what a horror I did see,
Nothing but a mushroom cloud surrounded all of me.
When it cleared, it got worse, the whole town wasn't there,
For miles and miles where I looked everything was bare.
Everyone that I loved and knew was lying on the ground,
It was so very strange there was not a single sound.
Everyone was gone and I could not say *goodbye*,
I was so very upset all I could do was cry.
It was the end of the world or so it would seem,
Oh what a very great relief it was all a silly dream.

Wendy Nugent (14) Our Lady's High School, Preston

MISCHIEF POEM

That's it the teacher's gone,
Up from our chairs we got one by one.
Across the class we dispersed.
To the board is where Gillian went first,
She threw it at William he threw it back
But look he's missed it hit the door with a smack
In walks the teacher,
And then she shouts get that smile off your face,
Or I'll send you out,
Now come on up who threw it first, .
You had better tell me or it will just make it worse.

Helen McDonnell (14) Our Lady's High School, Preston

DRUGS

Do you take drugs, and get high?
People do I don't know why.
They say they give them a buzz,
But do they know what it does?

They just laugh and think it's funny
Just to think of all that money.
Speed, Ecstasy, Crack and Dope,
They just haven't got a hope.

Then you start to cry and weep
'Cause you know you're in too deep.
Then you're in a hospital bed
And you just wish you were dead.

Lisa McGinty (14) Our Lady's High School, Preston

WINTER

Winter winds on the hills
Jack Frost freezes all the sills
Snow is falling in the street
Close the door keep in the heat.

Winter freezes chilly breezes
In the cold air hear sneezes.
Box of tissues being used.
Lots of cough sweets being chewed.

People blowing their blocked noses.
Taking medicine in big doses.
Doctors give patients prescriptions
This is the end of my winter description.

Lee Steel (12) Our Lady's High School, Preston

FREEDOM

They sit in the classroom,
You can see their faces,
You know they don't want to be there
They don't fit in,
No-one likes them, or so they think.
They want to be out in the open air,
Out of the stuffy classroom,
Away from everyone.
They are so lonely.

The bell rings for dinner,
A smile comes on their faces.
They can get out,
Out of the stuffy classroom,
Away from everyone.
They're free at last.
Free from everyone and everything
About stuffy school.
They feel happy,
They never want to go back.

They go to their secret place,
Hoping that no-one will find them.
They never go back to school.
Never again do they enter
They're free,
And that's the way it's going to stay.

Vicky Whittle (15) Our Lady's High School, Preston

THE GREAT SPELL

Hocus pocus I cast a spell,
The way I do it I will do it well,
A frog's eye,
A horse's leg,
A mouldy dog's tail,
And a rotten peg,
All mixed up into one pot,
Isn't it a good plot,
I'll need some blood, quite a lot,
Also that will go in the pot,
It all adds up to make to make one great spell,
I really hope it does sell,
I think that's enough in the pot,
Now it's an even better plot,
As I said before I'm going to sell it,
I really hope I make some profit,
I'll leave you now and go for a brew,
And prepare for the moment when I do,
Give it to the sampler which could be you.

Mark Foster (12) Our Lady's High School, Preston

THE GRANDFATHER CLOCK

Tick, tock, tock,
Goes the grandfather clock,
Chime, chime,
The bells ring in time,
The hands go round,
Round, round, round;
The big hand's pointing to the sky,
The little one to the ground.

It's six o'clock, it's dinner time!
We're just waiting for the chime, chime, chime!
Tick, tock, tick, tock, tick, tock, tick, tock,
Bong . . . Bong . . .
Hooray, horray!
it's fish, chips and peas for dinner today!

The school is boarded up and shut
The children are long gone;
And the grandfather clock is left alone,
To tick, tock, tick, tock on.

The clock had kept on going *bong*,
A few weeks after that,
But with no-one to hear him;
And no-one to wind him;
He didn't last very long.

Mark Cronin (12) Our Lady's High School, Preston

THE SIBERIAN TIGER

The Siberian tiger majestic and sleek
Proud and powerful prowling his beat
The silent stalker moves swiftly with skill
Pouncing his prey making a kill

The colourful creature camouflaged by day
Emerges at dusk hunting for prey
This fearsome feline endangered and rare
Hunted for his beautiful fur
Profit or pleasure they don't really care!

Katharine Reid (12) Our Lady's High School, Preston

JOSEPH MEANING JOE

When Joe was small,
he kicked and crawled
but soon he began to walk,
cups were smashed,
drinks were spilt
walls covered in chalk,
whilst mother screamed
and sister laughed
things became a muddle,
with puddles of juice
and hamsters on the loose
Joe was always in trouble.

Joanne McHugh (13) Our Lady's High School, Preston

THE GOBLIN

I am an evil goblin,
as evil as evil can be,
I turn people into stone,
if they get on the wrong side of me!
my toes are long and pointed,
my nose is double-jointed,
my eyes are black,
like a witch's cat,
if you don't like goblins,
you'd better stay in bed,
at twelve o'clock, midnight,
I turn people into gingerbread!

Clair Bottomley (11) Our Lady's High School, Lancaster

GOODBYE SUMMER, HELLO AUTUMN

Swirling, whirling, twirling around,
Leaves on the trees, leaves on the ground,
Most of them are red, brown and yellow,
The trees that they come from any at all,
The sizes just simply large, medium and small,
Some of them feel smooth and firm,
Whilst others are rough and feel quite tough.

Looking, searching, rooting for conkers,
Children in wellies,
Trousers and jumpers,
All of them wearing hats, scarves and gloves,
Trying to keep themselves nice and warm and snug.

Some days it's breezy,
Others it's calm.
Sometimes it's hot,
But mostly it's *cold*.

Charlotte Youren (11) Our Lady's High School, Lancaster

138

CAN'T YOU HEAR ME CALLING, LORD?

Can't you hear me calling, Lord?
Can't you hear my screams?
Can't you see me waiting for,
My most unwanted dreams?

Can I have the pain, Lord?
Give it as you will.
Make me cry and make me die,
An unhappy and wanted thrill.

I see the trouble I'd cause,
For my secret thrill.
The hatter and the chatter,
Would hit them like a drill.

When will the light come, Lord?
That shines so bright,
The dimness of my life,
The brightness of dark nights.

Should I slit my wrists, Lord?
Or a pistol to my head?
Should I hang myself upon,
A tight rope not just some thread?

Dreams of Heaven.
Dreams of light.
Dreams not to be told.
Dreams of flight.

Do you not know,
What I would do?
To be in Heaven
Alone with you?

Can't you hear me calling, Lord?
Can't you hear my screams?
Can't you see me waiting for,
My most unwanted dreams?

Sarah Kingston (14) Our Lady's High School, Lancaster

NOW I'M THIRTEEN

Now I'm thirteen
I've come to the age
Where all of my family
Want me in a cage.

I talk about boys
Much more than my toys
And mum buys me clothes
That I really loathe.

My dad is insane
My mum is a pain
And as for my sisters
They put me to shame

I give my friends *stick*
When they're on my *wick*
We end up in tears 'cos
We've boxed each other's ears.

Now, you know why
When I come of age
My parents go out
And buy me that cage!

Michelle Williams (13) Our Lady's High School, Lancaster

THE FOX HUNT

That animal was innocent,
It didn't deserve to die,
It shouldn't have gone that way,
It was screaming so loud I could cry.

The men on horses thought they were clever,
The men walking were looking for clues,
The dogs were just having fun,
The fox thought it had nothing to lose.

It was only looking for food,
They just appeared from behind,
She thought of her cubs back home,
But couldn't find anywhere to hide.

She ran not looking behind her,
But they soon caught up, she knew they would,
They grabbed her and threw her about,
Her skin was pierced and there was the first
Sign of blood.

They fought over her body,
Ripping her apart,
The men thought it was funny,
Laughing because they thought they were smart.

Then all the men set off for home,
Wondering what was for tea,
Leaving the fox unrecognisable,
The fox thought she was free.

That animal was innocent,
It didn't deserve to die,
People call it a sport,
But I call that a crime.

Kerry O'Hare (13) Our Lady's High School, Lancaster

141

THE EVERLASTING NIGHT

The sun slowly dropped from the skies,
Towards the swallowing waves,
And a transparent castle appears,
On the far side of the lagoon.

The moon winches itself up the velvet curtain,
Its powers of death, evil and hate grow.
The citadel becomes solid rock encased in mist.

The gargoyles on the turrets,
Come to life with evil glee,
And play their wicked games,
Of destroying the sun's work.

At the Gothic castle,
The goblins run and play,
They hide in the gargantuan hallways,
And hang the good creatures of the day.

Within the throne room,
The sorcerer conjured up,
A spell to make the castle last,
More than just a night.

He lacks the needed powers,
So he calls upon his wife,
The evil Lady Morganer, Queen of Death.

She whips her evil wand,
And in the air the images of sun and moon appear,
So with the powers of her hellish husband,
She destroys the sun and its image.

On the throne they sit,
The King of Hell and the Queen of Death,
And the sun never rises,
So the fort lives on.

Michael Lewis (13) Our Lady's High School, Lancaster

BOTTLES

I drink to forget
I forgot to stop drinking
reality, my dear is a crippling bore
I'm a sickening wretch
with a national debt
to pay off in *hangover* cures

Got a head full of bottles
and eyes full of glass
This drink is my first and my last

I'm going down on this ship
down on this bursting vessel
put gin in my drip
bring *Jack Daniels* to my jail cell

Got a head full of bottles
and eyes full of glass
this drink is my first and my last.

Liam Dawson (13) Our Lady's High School, Lancaster

THE OFFICE CLERK

Bonded with the books with which he worked
Up popped the head of the furnished clerk
Eyes wandering round the enclosed chamber
The dim gazing eyes stumble upon
The secretary, Miss Turn-on.

His eyes worked her body
Until they were drained.
Over the silk mini skirt he did ponder
Wondering whether to walk over yonder.

Her stream line curves oh he desires
And those smooth waxed legs did he admire.
With the wind in her hair cruising along
She would move to a hot new song.

Up they would go in a swift new jet
Off to a place where his wife couldn't get.
There they would bask under the scorching sun
Both messing about and having some fun.
The pair would climb the stairs
When all of a sudden the telephone blares.

The clerk awoke from his Monday fancy
No more jet and no more sun,
His lunch time fantasy came to a close.
But Miss Turn-on still sat there eating her bun
Filling the hole in her ever increasing tum.

Philip McGlone (13) Our Lady's High School, Lancaster

FEAR OF THE DARK

Darkness is a witch's hat,
Everlasting doom in black,
Darkness so dark you cannot see,
The menacing ghosts giggle with glee.
Darkness is silence no sound at all,
Darkness a pit with an everlasting fall,
Darkness is cold like an ice queen's wand,
So cold it freezes the desolate pond,
Darkness is cruelty in which you get hurt,
As you lie in bed freezing in your shirt,
Darkness is sadness from your eye comes a tear,
You release from your vault your darkest fear.
Darkness in your mind,
Searching lost memories you'll never find,
Light at last, the silence is gone,
Warmth has come, darkness is done.

Alex Turner (12) Our Lady and St John RC High School

FEAR OF DARKNESS

Fear of darkness
When all alone.
Fear of darkness
When in a room on your own.

Fear of darkness
When you've had a bad dream.
Fear of darkness
When the lamp doesn't gleam.

Fear of darkness
When you've turned out the light.
Fear of darkness
When it's gone midnight . . .

Amanda Holden (12) Our Lady and St John RC High School

DETENTION IN THE DARK

I know I should have paid attention,
but it's all John Smith's fault I'm in detention.
Nothing to watch but those tall black clouds,
rising above the football crowds.
A roll of thunder, a flash of light,
I nearly died of darkness fright.
Those rats scurrying here and there,
of course they're not *really* there.
Sitting here on a dark afternoon,
I can almost see the light of the moon.
Is that a ghost I see before me?
Oh, no it's a shadow of a tree.
Oh what joy when a teacher hums.
Next time I'll run when darkness comes.

Stephen Johnston (12) Our Lady and St John RC High School

MOON WARRIOR

What's that coming, through the sky?
With wild, long hair and fire in eye.
A black, black horse - as dark as night
A golden chariot ablaze with light
A messenger from the moon
Who spreads the word of lasting doom

If you look up to the sky
And see the moon
He's near by.

Daniel Hodgson (13) Our Lady and St John RC High School

FEAR

Lightning and thunder from the skies,
Creepy crawlies, spiders, flies.

Darkness swallows those who come near,
Silence smothers those who show fear.

Footsteps echo from behind,
Are they real or in my mind?

A cry of anguish freezes my heart,
Piercing it through like a flying dart.

But these are childish fantasies I should
Have left them all behind,
None of them are real and yet they're
Lodged forever in my mind.

Emma Greaves (12) Our Lady and St John RC High School

DARKNESS!

As dark as a heart without any soul
As dark as the deepest blackest black hole
As dark as the thunder in a cloud filled sky
The evilest deceit the most wicked lie
As dark as the world without any light
As dark as the forest on a winter's night
As dark as a dungeon without a key
As dark as an eye that cannot see
This place would be scary day and night
If there was only darkness never any light.

Debbie Inward (13) Our Lady and St John RC High School

PEACE?

Belfast such a pretty town,
Yet one thing spoils it so,
The wars amongst the people,
But why? I want to know.

Religion is the problem,
Because they cannot see,
That people have the privilege
Of who they want to be.

The shooting and the bombing,
The grief within us all,
But no-one takes much notice
Of the big redbrick *peace* wall.

Then, the protests started
Banners reading *Stop the war*
All the people hoping that
There wouldn't be anymore.

But on the News one morning,
What everyone wanted to hear,
Peter Smith announced that:-
The violence all ends here!

Emma Brown (12) Our Lady and St John RC High School

148

MY BEST THINGS

Being at the airport before my holidays,
Don't get too excited, my dad always says.
Getting lots of money for my birthday,
Then going out and spending it, the very next day.
Having a warm shower after playing football in the rain and the mud,
Then sitting down to a nice jacket spud.
The nice big rock buns that I made.
The taste of Lucozade.
Being the captain of the school football team,
And falling asleep into a nice deep dream.
My mum's hot and spicy curry,
They make you go to the toilet, in such a hurry.
Chinese food on a Saturday night.
Watching Lennox Lewis have a good fight.
I could go on for ever and ever.

Matthew Baldwin (12) Our Lady and St John RC High School

NOVEMBER LAKE

One frozen morning, sleepy lake greets,
As naked branches sway in lifeless unison.
Fresh cotton clouds pass smoothly above
Quietly
So nothing awakes.
Absent nests hang loosely in Mother's cradle,
All joyful life still to be slowly awakened.
Till springtime arrives.
Hush lake, sleep,
Beauty sleep, till winter's spell departs.

James Whalley (15) Park High School

LACHLARN'S NOVEMBER

The crooning often slurred its choral
Its pitiful solemnity wafted on the wind.
I pondered on its forgotten song.
In Lachlarn,
The crisp carousel
Of autumn's past still lingered in the cobbled lanes
Entwined in November's harsh and grasping brashness.
Tendrils of willow
and ivy
Crept down the sidewalk of Hebden End

And beyond the brook, stark silhouettes
Of birch and horse chestnut shamelessly cried from cold.
The wind carried seasonal smells of
Humbugs and
Candy as it weaved
Its way down Peddler's Track and up Brogdin Lane.
I meandered through my memories of toasting
Forks and hot ladles
Preserves of
The blacksmith and baker, tanner and weaver.

The first candles littered the windows
And as the mist enveloped the broad
Mill chimney
And shrouded the church
Tower in the swirls of familiar silence
I climbed where Blackthorn turns white to gaze upon
The aura
Of my sleeping town
Gleaming with the first flakes of winter.

Abigail Driver (15) Park High School

NOVEMBER NIGHT

It was an early November night.
That cold crisp air beckoned me to stray from inside.
The smoky smell brought back memories,
Long ago,
From my childhood days.
I glanced at the village and scattered where fires,
Giving off heat to the small crowd that gathered there.
All orange and bright,
A picture.
I went to find a welcoming fire.

I wandered through the desolate streets.
A carpet of crisp colourful leaves lined the paths.
The cold breath poured from my nose and mouth.
The clear air.
A wonderful night.
The fireworks went off and lit up the dark night sky,
Showers of colourful rain streamed onto my head.
A mixture of smells.
Breathtaking.
Steaming soup, plot toffee and hot dogs.

As the evening drew to a finish,
The fireworks stopped and the moon and stars lit the sky.
The orange fires were getting smaller.
The night light,
The stars shining bright.
Full of spirits people walked home in cheerful groups.
The atmosphere was warm although the air was cold.
My scarf kept me warm.
I went home.
Bonfire night early in November.

Rachel Hardman (15) Park High School

AN AUTUMN DAWN

Moonbeams dance on the sparkling stream
While foamy waves gently break on the pebbled beach.
The autumn leaves sway in the sea breeze
Bright by day
Dull in dark night - time
The striking crimsons, golds and yellows are now black,
The cold night reflected by the icy cold sea.
Sealife stirs in the
Murky pools
As the sun rises above the hills.

Janine Thompson (14) Park High School

THE MANSION

High upon a dark cliff it stands.
An eerie shadow creeps across the lands
An owl hoots, a bat swoops by
An evil creature lets out a sigh.
Lightning strikes, the sky is bright.
Then in a split second, again it is night.

The sun rises up into the sky
Then you gaze up ever so high
A different house stand there now
How it has happened you don't know how.
No misty mansion do you see
But a stately house locked up with a key.

Peter Odor (11) Park High School

152

THE NIGHT I THOUGHT GHOSTS HAD PAID A VISIT

Ghosts are frightening, scary and creepy.
They roam around people's houses from evening to dawn.
Making noises, opening doors, making children's rooms go cold
They've decided to visit my house tonight, they're creeping around
                                                            downstairs.
Why couldn't they have gone next door?
They've already got to my cat, I heard her yelp.
I wish the light of day would come.
They've found the fridge, I can hear the munching, thank God their
                                                            bait is not me.
I pray and hope they don't find the knives.
They're coming upstairs, I'm next in line.
Oh please will you spare me I'm thinking.
They open the door, I try to scream but nothing will come out
Don't panic I think, don't panic.
'Sarah,' they shout, 'what are you doing?'
I mumble, 'I'm hiding from you.'
They're coming closer, I think of something to say as my last words
They throw back the blanket, I find my scream
Ahhhhhh Ahhhhhh
'Sarah,' they shout, 'don't be scared it's me.'
I look up to find that standing over me is someone not scary but . . .
My dad . . . phew!

Sarah Foster (11) Park High School

HALLOWE'EN

On a broomstick bound for Pendle,
There's a witch with a mournful eye,
Witches hats and big black cats,
Flashing by in the misty sky.

How the witches laugh, they laugh with all their might,
Ha, ha, ha, ha, ha,
Laugh and laugh the whole night through,
And half the hallowe'en night.

Witches witches witches witches,
Witches witches witches whooo,
Witches witches witches witches,
They will cast a spell on you.

        Boo!

Jodi Carlisle (11) Park High School

THE WITCH

See the witch with a big black hat,
She's got a broomstick, she's got a cat,
She'll be comin' to your door this very hallowe'en
So don't you dare think it's just a dream.

See her bats flying in the air
If I were you I'd beware.
'Cos she's comin' real soon
She's packing her suitcase, her cloak and her broom.

Flying through the sky with her cape lurking behind her.
She's got that feeling that she's going to find yer!
So watch out
'Cos the old witch is about.

Gina Sarfas (11) Park High School

GHOSTS

A sharp intake of breath,
I sit up suddenly.
Was that the creak of something wooden?

A tree outside,
My spirits soar,
Or a step on a floorboard outside my door?

I go to the window,
The moon's shining bright,
Like a guiding star or a warning light.

I hear footsteps approaching,
I try to scream out loud,
But nothing comes out, not even a sound.

I see faces all around,
They laugh and they jeer,
I don't know what to do I'm enveloped in fear.

The darkness is closing,
I collapse on the floor.
For the evil has triumphed for forever more.

They found me next morning,
On the bed,
No known cause of death the doctor said.

Sarah Hesketh (11) Park High School

THE NIGHT LIGHT

The night lamp burnt through the bleak night's mist.

Alone in the empty street, with occasional
Car lights or call of a watchful owl,

Standing bright,
With only keen moths
To linger fluttering amid the orange beam.

As dawn breaks, the silence disappears and light floods
In from the crisp skies.

Obsolete,
It stands alone, unnoticed once more.

Laura Wightman (14) Park High School

A POEM IN AUTUMN

Early it was that autumn morning
The quaint sound of crisp, cold leaves crackling underfoot
And the mighty, moss-masked bridge of stone
Solitary.
Under this, a stream
Where the weary willow weeped and the birds sang,
The sweet smell of flowers, captured in morning dew.
A cautious cat passed
Unaware
The once dead town was now wakening.

John McCaul (14) Park High School

WINTER

Awoken by the morning's silence
My bleary eyes opened, to a blanket of white.
Snowflakes tumbled and turned to the ground
Where, as boys
We had played for hours,
In the snow, slipping, sliding, shouting and screaming.
Water dripped from icicles, like tears from the eye
Slowly trickling
Down my cheeks
Till I taste the day on my blue lips.

Beth Turley (15) Park High School

WINTER SUNSET

The sun was setting behind the hills,
A great glowing jewel set in the red, evening sky,
Growing darker, its light fading away,
So quickly
As I watched in awe.
The icy wind sang sweet lullabies to the trees,
And softly combed through the blades of grass.
The sun smiled and gave
A last wink,
And sank into the cold winter's night.

Tracy Wilkinson (14) Park High School

SPRING SEASHORE

Dew dropped daisies (flickering fried eggs)
Silver hillside, silver sea, shimmering sunshine
Seagulls circling high in the sky
Loving lambs
Leaping lively
White horses swiftly splashing on the rocks
Below
Another beginning to another spring day
The life-giving flow
Of the sea
The sun, the sea, for eternity.

Catherine Hall (14) Park High School

CLOSE TO THE EDGE

The fading rays of the setting sun
Reach out to touch me with their radiant fingers
Before slipping away to darkness.
Silent stars
In the cold heavens
Pierce the cloak of night like diamonds; the perfect crown.
Standing on the headland I am now powerless
As the elements
Duel in the
Crushing conflict of eternity.

Deborah Stansfield (14) Park High School

158

ZOO POEM

I am a lion in a Belgium zoo.
I have a scar on my head,
And a loose tooth too
For two years of suffering, is quite enough,
And the wind is coming into the cage rough and tough.
I am freezing and in pain,
And out of shelter from the rain,
I am scared and hungry,
With a rumbling pain in my stomach,
I miss my family,
I miss the wild,
I wish I was dead and in heaven.

I hear laughing in the smoky distance
My eyes are hurting and I'm almost blind,
I could do with beefy lovely zebra
But all I have to eat is old crumbly biscuits
I have no energy to growl or walk,
I have no mates to have a talk.
The zoo keeper really is a nasty guy
All I have to say is just to cry.
The floor of the cages are really slimy
With green slimy horrible nasty goo.

Darren Kirkham (12) Parklands High School

SOMEONE ELSE'S WAR!

With bombs dropping all around,
Exploding when they hit the ground,
Love and war just do not mix.
The destruction here you cannot fix.

Every time a person cries,
Somewhere else a person dies,
Will they live to tell the tales,
Or will they die, their mission fails?

People hungry in the street,
Insufficient food to eat,
How someone lives to tell the story,
Of war and famine, hope and glory.

Carla Hayes (12) Parklands High School

MY MARVELLOUS MEAL

Melon as fresh as morning
dew,
Cherries tasting so very
new.
Steak as tender as a
mother's care,
Corn the colour of golden
hair.

Knickerbocker glory as tall
as a mountain,
A bit of white wine as
cold as a fountain
Cheese and crackers at
the end,
I like to eat them with
a friend!

Sarah Masheter (11) Parklands High School

160

THE MAGIC GARDEN

When I was a little girl,
Of about five years old
My nanna told me lots of things,
Especially stories of gold,

But my favourite one,
The one I loved best,
Was about a garden made of sweets,
And all sorts like chocolate birds' nests

There was a lemonade lake,
With fish made of jelly,
And when I ate the fish,
They wriggled in my belly!

Each blade of grass is made from chocolate,
Each tree made from candy floss,
The soil made from jelly beans,
And oh! The tasty liquorice moss.

Another thing nanna said,
Was a tree made from honey
And if you were good,
It turned into money!

Just imagine that money for your mum and dad
I always used to say 'How?'
But nanna's good at telling stories,
It's a shame I don't believe them now!

Gemma Hodkinson (12) Parklands High School

MY NAN TOLD ME!

My Nan told me stories,
When I went to sleep,
I found it very much better,
Better than counting sheep.

She told me tales of Peter Pan,
And of Captain Hook,
But the great thing about my Nan was,
She didn't read a book.

Her stories were so lively
Even though they'd differ,
When she told me something scary
It made my spine shiver.

She told me tales of teddy bears,
And of little Noddy
Her stories are so good that,
I need to tell somebody.

I tell my little sister,
When she's safe in bed,
I like to think that the stories,
Stay up in her head.

I don't believe them now,
The tales my Nan told,
But I think that's only,
Because I've grown so *old*!

Geraldine Morey (12) Parklands High School

STORY TIME

The young boy
snuggles down into
his soft, warm covers.
Briefly, he looks at the snow
piling up in the corners of the
wooden window frame. His mother's
voice changes, his mind tunes back
into the story, heard many times
over. Her child watches lovingly,
happily, eyes feeling heavy,
drooping, closing. The mother
shuts and places the book down
and slowly and silently leaves.
She turns for a last look
at her child sleeping
peacefully. She
smiles and pulls
the door
shut.

Iain Jackson (12) Parklands High School

THE TUNES OF ORPHEUS AND THE SIRENS

Dig your oars deep, me lads, thrust them at the sea.
For while ever we row this boat, me lads,
There's hope for you and me.
A sailor's life is never lost whilst other men are free.
So dig your oars deep me lads, thrust them at the sea.

Sleep awhile my sailor boy, relax and rest your head
Calm beneath the rippling waves, upon the soft sea bed.
Slumber deep my sailor boy, let me soothe your brow
Leave behind your earthly traits and dwell with the sirens now.

Jennifer Worthington (13) Priory High School, Penwortham

THE SNOW

I awoke one morning to silence,
Unusual I thought,
But when I opened my curtains,
I found the reason why -
Snow!
Falling steadily,
Falling constantly,
Falling silently,
It covered the ground,
Making it look like an uncoloured drawing,
It filled the sky,
It filled the ground,
The silence was audible,
And unlike life
There wasn't a footprint or mark in the white covering

Paul Duckworth (13) Priory High School, Penwortham

STREET WANDERER

As he's standing in the middle of the road,
You can see his bright blue and green feathers shining.
The traffic is building up behind him
Beep, beep go the car horns
As he moved from the road I threw him some bread.
He bends his long, slender neck carefully to pick up the bread.
He takes his time like he's trying not to break his neck.
He raises his tail feathers up high
Just like the shape of a fan
But when a cat comes
One *squawk* and Percy the peacock will run away.

Ruth Halstead (12) Priory High School, Penwortham

THING

It's a black diamond night.
The moon glinting in the midnight sky
Like a silver medallion
Everything's quiet, nothing stirs nothing moves
It's like the night before Christmas
Then someone gets up creaking along the floor to the toilet
It comes back it's my dad
Silence again
Next the stairs start creaking one by one
A figure comes on to the bottom of the stairs
To the kitchen door but before it can reach the door
A quiet and mysterious voice cries
'Get out of the house'
He looks up
There's a figure in a shadow holding a massive knife
Then silence
Next morning dad's gone everyone's crying
That night at twelve o'clock
With a moon like a toenail in the sky
A figure appears in the house
And then with a big shriek
The house disappears
With me with it.

Matthew Procter (13) Priory High School, Penwortham

AUTUMN

Autumn is the time of year,
Things start to die and winter's near,
Leaves begin to fall off trees,
Rain and wind, no gentle breeze,
Conkers fall from chestnut trees,
Acorns, nuts and ash keys,
Leaves in crimson, red and brown,
Green and yellow come swirling down,
Harvest comes and goes so quick,
There's damsons, pears and apples to pick,
Hallowe'en the spooky night,
Fireworks and bonfires bright,
Then it's over, Christmas is near,
Farewell to autumn, winter's here.

Gillian Foster (12) Priory High School, Penwortham

THE SONG OF THE SIRENS

Orpheus:
Look to the left boys, look to the right
Pull on the oars boys, with all your might:
Watch for the tides
And watch for the spray
Full speed we're sailing
On our way.

Sirens:
Come to me for rest
Come to me for sleep
Come to me for safety - from the deep

Look to the left boys
No, come to me for rest
Look to the right boys
No, come to me for sleep
Pull on the oars boys
Come to me for safety
From the perils of the deep.
Watch for the spray
That's it boys, we are on our way.

Richard Henfield (13) Priory High School, Penwortham

MY FAVOURITE SEASON

My favourite season's autumn
When the leaves fall from the trees,
Oranges, reds, browns and yellows,
The horse chestnut just sits there swaying in the breeze
Its spiky green coat protecting it
One strong gust of wind and the chestnut crashes to the ground
The pure white inside is revealed like cotton wool wrapped
                                            around a treasure
Then the shiny brown chestnut is visible.

Elaine Butler (14) Priory High School, Penwortham

WINTER

Water from frosty stalactites drop,
Rivers at their bridges stop.
Every minute, an hour
Grass becomes hard as metal,
From the heavens, snow cascades
Each a pearl-white petal.

Spinning jennies, leaves in
Mid air gyrate,
Squirrel and dormouse hibernate,
Ice encrusted leaves weigh
Down the gutter,
The car ignites with cough and splutter.

Dogs at backdoor kennels bark,
Trees now jagged along the skyline
Stark,
Devoid of leaf stand,
The icy wind their cape,
Crisp snow has blanketed
The desolate landscape.

Sarah Preisner (13) Priory High School, Penwortham

168

STICKS AND STONES

You look at me and make judgement,
I hear the words flow as easily as water from a tap,
You don't understand my pain, do you?
For every syllable is like a dagger in my heart,
Stabbing harder, deeper every time.
No physical scars you leave,
But mental scars are left,
My feelings are hurt,
But you will never understand,
Eventually I hear it so much and
Like a child being told not to do something,
It sinks in.
And then I go home to my place of rest,
Take the sharpest of the knives,
Look at it for a final lingering moment,
Then in a fit of madness,
Stab . . . stab . . . stab . . . then darkness
I am no more.

Lisa Clements (13) Priory High School, Penwortham

WINTER

Winter is the time of year
That most folks hate.
But I relish crisp dry mornings
and logs burning in the grate.
And nice warm beds on chilly nights
and steaming cups of tea
With bonfire night and fireworks
and sticky treacle toffee.
Yes snow and ice to me are nice
not sunny days in the lakes.
So let's have icicles and frost
Winter time is best for me!

Matthew Burton (12) Priory High School, Penwortham

WASH, WASH!

Clothes, clothes,
Long and short
Dirty again, clean again,
After each wash.

Scrub, scrub
Or tumble dry
Spinning round,
Like a whizzing mind.

Swish, swish
The water goes
Shaking and erupting like a volcano
It *explodes!*

Until slowly it's exhausted
'I'm tired,' it replies
Slowing down its speed
Wearing away the sound
Obtaining peace and silence.

Anita Vaza (12) Priory High School, Penwortham

AUTUMN

In autumn time the trees are bare
And leaves are scattered everywhere.
A golden blanket covers the ground
And underneath horse chestnuts can be found.

Autumn mists start creeping in
And the birds flight south
Will soon begin.

Nesting animals start to prepare
For the long time ahead
When food won't be spare.

Sarah Durant (12) Priory High School, Burscough

THE FOUL

Football is a game for hard nuts,
Only wimps don't play.
Only the ref keeps you apart
Until the next day.
Oh, no! Bad tackle! Just rushed in,
I think it's a booking, I don't blame him.
The boy he tackled, nerd in school,
Flat on his back in a muddy pool.
Teacher came over, looked at me
I said, 'Sir don't look at me,
He did it, him over there!'
The boy who did it just stood there -
He looked at me and punched the air!

Andrew Crosbie (12) Priory High School, Burscough

FRIENDS

The old horse clomped over to the little
Donkey
His eyes gentle and restful.
His hairy feet were covered with dried mud,
His woolly fur was dirty.
The donkey raised his head slowly.
It was becoming dusk, the air was peaceful,
They chatted for a while,
Scratched each other's back
And twitched at the flies.
Their tails swished and their ears pricked
As a voice called out from the fence;
They both wandered side by side to the
Fence
They were led to their stalls,
Watered and fed
And left for the night ahead.

Ruth Belshaw (12) Priory High School, Burscough

THE COUNTRYSIDE

On the breeze the flowers bob
The thin green stems
And the bright coloured tops
Swaying, swaying to and fro
The pretty coloured flowers they do blow.

Along the stream and over fall
The pea pod boats
Hesitate and stall
Bob, bob babbling up, up and around
The pea pod boats sail merrily down.

Katie Diane Halsall (13) Priory High School, Burscough

COLOURS

Blue is the sea that swishes about,
Yellow are flowers without a doubt,
Green is the grass, fresh on a farm,
Red is the blood when you cut your arm,
Pink is a cushion on a chair,
White is the colour of the clouds in the air.

Peter Langley (12) Priory High School, Burscough

AUTUMN

The golden leaves that fall on the ground,
Red, yellow, orange or brown.
Crackle, crunch, crisp and rustle,
The children love it, they sing and whistle.

They love kicking them here and there,
Until the trees, all turn bare.
It's a sign for winter is coming,
The weather will be dull and snowing.

They'll love the snow as much as the leaves,
They'll remember them by all the bare trees.
Autumn is a colourful season,
No-one can hate it, there are no reasons.

Ricktha Miah (12) Priory High School, Burscough

HE KNOWS THE DANGERS

Behind the bike shed he was, behind the bike shed,
In a gang he was, in a gang,
Smoking he was, smoking,
Made him splutter it did, made him splutter,
Why does he smoke, why?
You can get lung cancer you can, lung cancer,
Does he want to live long, does he?
He knows the dangers he does, he knows the dangers,
It makes him look big it does, makes him look big,
Will he be big when he's lying in a hole, will he?

Claire Hale (12) Priory High School, Burscough

THE INSECTS

The sting of a wasp,
It can be lethal!
It hurts like heck
And it isn't gleeful.

The spider's web,
It catches flies.
He chews them up
And spits out the eyes!

The sound of a cricket
It wakes people up;
It drinks lots of water
Without a cup!

The wee little cockroach,
It gets on people's nerves;
It eats their dinner
And doesn't like the herbs!

Ian Williams (12) Priory High School, Burscough

SPIDERS

Black and furry,
Eight legs and scary,
Creeping about in your bath tub,
They hide and sneak,
Make cobwebs in your loft,
That is the spider!

Paul Blythin (13) Priory High School, Burscough

175

ENGLISH WEATHER

Everyone's playing happily outside,
Now it's started raining they'll have to come inside.
Grounds get wet,
Lakes get high,
If I look up I will see a black sky,
Sunshine's back again, hip hip hooray,
Hope it stays for the rest of the day.

We can go outside again to play,
Everyone wondering how long the sunshine will stay,
And now it's starting to rain,
The thunder and lightning is starting again,
Hiding under my bedcover away from the rain,
Everyone has now come inside,
Really there aren't enough places to hide.

Gemma Cox (12) Priory High School, Burscough

THE BLOW OF THE SNOW

The blow of the snow is icy cold,
Just like shivery gleaming gold.
It comes in flakes and groups of eight.
Zip up your coat or you'll get a cold,
In the shivery, shivery icy snow.

Lynne Butterworth (12) Priory High School, Burscough

GIVE UP SMOKING

Smoking is a dirty habit,
Kick it whilst you can.
Makes your fingers all yellow,
should be given a ban!

Smoking can give you lung cancer,
Heart disease and smelly breath too.
So do yourself a big favour,
And flush your cigarettes down the loo.

Cheryl Pallett (12) Priory High School, Burscough

THE ENCHANTER

Like enchanted woods,
I hear you, I feel you,
Yet you're nowhere to be seen.

Like an enchanted fairy,
I dance like you, I fly like you,
Yet I have no wings.

Like an enchanted dragon,
You seem fierce, and sound fierce,
Yet you are kind and warm-hearted.

Like enchanted horses,
I hear you canter,
I see you canter for, yes you are,
My one and only enchanter.

Jennie Comber (12) Priory High School, Burscough

THE MAN FROM JAPAN

Once there was a man from Japan,
who rolled down a hill in a pan,
when he hit a rock,
he had a shock,
he found himself in Pakistan.

Matthew Wright (12) Priory High School, Burscough

THE GIFTS OF NATURE

A new-born lamb struggling to stand,
An injured hedgehog in a helping hand.
A baby bird trying to survive,
Working bees in a bee hive.

Mother Nature blows the breeze,
And gives small animals warmth in the trees.
She gives them branches, twigs and feathers,
To stand up to the cold winter weather.

Sea creatures live under the sand,
Under the water and not on the land.
Big fishes, little fishes all swimming free,
In their own little world under the sea.

Look after our planet and don't be a fool,
Don't pollute the air with your car fuel.
This planet takes care of you,
So make an effort to look after it too.

Amy Dunn (12) Priory High School, Burscough

THE SUN

The sun is high up in the sky,
So round, so bright, so bold,
I wonder how long it's been there?
It must be very old.

Every time I look in the sky,
I catch a glimpse of the sun in my eye,
Half the day it's out to play,
Then the other half comes and frightens it away.

The sun helps us, the world to see,
How full of life the world must be,
It must be very powerful to shine,
And make the trees and plants so fine.

It must stop turning,
It must stop burning,
Someday, somehow,

And when it does, we will all be doomed,
Because our lives will be full of gloom.

Sally Smith (12) Priory High School, Burscough

HOMELESS IN THE SUBWAY

Alone in the dark and damp and drab
I sit with a bowl for begged pennies.
Sadness and pain is around me, within me.
Then I hear the noise of an approaching train.
Steam hisses, the train slows to a standstill,
People leap off while others step on.
They push and shove to get out in the open
Ignoring me.

A small girl points at me but her mum hurries past.
My chilled bare knee gets kicked in the flurry.
The smell of diesel shoots into my nostrils and makes me dizzy.
My head falls back on to the wall decorated with graffiti,
As the train pulls off and round another dark corner.
The subway is clear except for a few stragglers.
Crisp packets and wrappers rustle and whirl in a corner.
I push my dirty, raggy hair out of my face
And try to squeeze my eyes to sleep.

A warm, dry hand presses a cool, round shape into my dirty fist.
I raise my eyes to meet hers.
She smiles back down.
'Buy something nice,' she says,
And trundles off with shopping trolley behind her.
Here's today's food sorted, but what about tomorrow?

Sarah Holman (13) Priory High School, Burscough

A WHOLE NEW DAY

The day was new,
The sky was blue,
A whole new day came into view.
The birds were singing,
Church bells ringing,
A whole new day was here.

Animals were all around,
In the trees and on the ground,
Children having lots of fun,
The smell of freshly baked new buns,
I could hear people calling,
Babies down the streets were bawling.

A girl was playing in the street,
Her brother standing by her feet,
'Come on in, the fire is lit,
Come and warm your toes a bit.'
It was cold, the day was old,
A whole new day was done.

Joanne Partridge (12) Priory High School, Burscough

SEA JOURNEY

If I could travel the ocean blue,
These are the things that I would do.
Swim with the puffins under the sea,
Fly with the seagulls and search for my tea.
Dive with the dolphins who have such a lark,
And hurry home quick 'cos it's getting quite dark.
Wake up in the morning get over my yawning,
And go down the beach and play.
I'll get in my boat and set out afloat on a
Warm and sunny day.
I watch the fight of a shark and a whale,
And then pop to the surface and it was blowing a gale.
I'll go back to the bottom and lean on a rock,
Good heavens it's nearly 12 o'clock.
I'll ride with the dolphins and get out at the dock,
Shake off the water and by that time it's 12 o'clock.

Suzanne Cocks (12) Priory High School, Burscough

THE STORM

The waves come crashing on the shore,
The clouds are threatening more and more,
A storm is brewing.

The water smashes against the rocks,
The wind and rain runs amok,
The thunder roars and the lightning cracks.

The rain has stopped, the wind moves on,
The storm is dying and will soon be gone,
The angry sea is calm once more.

James Norris (13) Priory High School, Burscough

TEA TIME

Spaghetti bolognese tonight, or was it stew?
Is it really only three, or half past two?
I can't remember what I had for lunch.
Oh yeah, egg butt (with a crunch).
I'm longing for my tea.
Yes, it's only three.

Mum says I seem to eat a lot for someone of my age.
But if I don't get something soon I'll get into a rage.
I'm longing for my tea.
Is it really only three?

Jane Ashley (14) Rhyddings High School

LONELY PRINCE

Alone in the house again
it's the same every day,
my parents are out greeting people
while the guards stand earning their pay.

When my parents are in they're too busy
to do the normal stuff they should,
they give me everything I want
but what I really want is love.

I'm not looking forward to being King
being out every minute of the day,
people glaring and waving
people shouting, 'Look, it's the King.'

People think I'm happy
being what I am,
but underneath I'm lonely
as lonely as anyone could ever be.

Louise Paintin (15) Rhyddings High School

THE MORNING

Woke up in the morning
As tired as can be
Wanting to be back in bed
Watching the BBC.

Having to walk to school
In the pouring rain
Wanting to be back in bed
Playing a computer game.

Walking through the school gates
And being late for class
Wanting to be back in bed
And let the whole day pass.

Dinner time is over
My eyes are almost shut
Wanting to be back in bed
With a delicious chip butt.

It's almost hometime
I can't wait to get home
I want to be back in bed
All cosy and warm.

Ross Mackey (14) Rhyddings High School

I MISS TONI

I miss Toni
Without her life is lonely -
I look at her empty house.
Nobody there not even a mouse.

I think about her all the time,
Without her life doesn't shine.
We knew each other since we were three.
She really meant a lot to me.

I remember all the good times.
When we used to sit down,
And drink chocolate milk
And make up story rhymes.

I now regret all the arguments we had,
It was mostly me just being bad.

I really, really miss her.

Joanne Mainon (12) Rhyddings High School

MY GREAT GRAN

She sits there
In her chair,
thinking of the days gone by.

In the window seat she sits.
She's the spy,
Thinking of the days gone by.

No longer is she strong,
As the mornings go along.
Waves to the papergirl.
Waves to the milkman.
Waves to the postman,
Waves to the dustman.
All the people that pass her by.

As she sits there
In her chair,
Thinking of the days gone by.

Ruth Williams (12) Rhyddings High School

SCHOOL'S OUT

I'm longing for the bell to go
I'm dying to get out.
I'm getting hot and flustered,
I really want to shout.
School's out!

Time's ticking by it's 5 past 3
The teacher's babblin' on
But I'm not payin' attention you see,
Because in 5 mins I'll be gone.

It's time to put the stools up,
And coats are flying round,
the teacher says, 'Be quiet please'
There's not a single sound.

We're stood behind our tables
Waiting for the end to come,
The bell went, the doors open,
And everyone starts to run!

Emma Grundy (14) Rhyddings High School

BLACK AND WHITE

The black twists and turns
blending with the white.
Shapes like ghosts
float about the paper.
Dark, black shadows
creep towards me howling.

Tom Jeffs (11) Ribblesdale High School

WAR - AS A SOLDIER SEES IT

Land torn in half,
Soldiers crawling on the ground,
Hatred and despair hangs in the air,
And there are decaying bodies of men, women and children
scattered around.

How do you explain the eight year old boy, that's just shot
your best friend?
Or the feeling of killing a man only to discover that it's a woman?
How will we survive to the bitter end?

All this is caused by anger and greed,
War doesn't prove anything, only how cruel man can be,
So hear our plea,
Forgive and forget before it's too late,
Before your voice is lost in the darkness and despair that
hangs in the air.

Nicola Johnson (14) Ribblesdale High School

THE FOUR SEASONS

Spring is the time for all things new
Seeds are bursting forth
Pairs of birds do bill and coo
The wind's not from the north.

Summer's here all green and bright
The time when bees buzz by
Longer days and shorter nights
And swallows in the sky.

Autumn's the time that leaves will fall
Time for the rain to come
Birds will feel warm countries call
Flying south to the warming sun

Winter the season that snow falls from the sky
The time we go spotting pheasants
The time we eat our Christmas pie
And Santa brings our presents.

Sarah Kwasniewski (12) Ribblesdale High School

MRS POOLE

It was a Monday morning,
And I was on my way to school,
I looked at my timetable,
It said *Mrs Poole!*

I shivered all over,
Up and down,
She's the worst teacher,
She looks just like a hound!

She stood there with
A nasty grin,
I would be very surprised
If she had any kin.

The worst thing is
I have to say,
She's never going
To go away!

Holly Woodworth (11) Ribblesdale High School

MY PET

Animals, noisy all around
Which should I choose?
A dog that barks
A snake, hiss! hiss!
A jumping frog that croaks!
But when I'd looked in every cage but one
I saw a baby hamster
Small, grey and white it was
Just the pet for me!

Stephanie Swift (11) St John Fisher & Thomas More RC
High School

COUNTRYSIDE HAPPENINGS

I was standing outside my house one night,
Observing my surroundings,
A group of hills outlined the sky,
The valley slept while clouds went by.

Morning was welcomed with drops of dew,
Small animals awakened to start anew,
A nearby thrush sang a song,
It was perched on an oak tree firm and strong.

I watched some more as it swooped to the ground.
I crept closer to see what it had found.
Perhaps an insect or a worm?
Whatever it was, it knew how to squirm!

As the day drew on, the light seemed to fade.
Animals went to their burrows, their beds ready-made,
I decided to retire for the night.
I would watch them tomorrow when it became light.

Helen Shoesmith (13) St John Fisher & Thomas More
High School

ROSES

R ed, the colour that speaks
O f mysteries and madness.
S unsets blush on eastern skies,
E tna's smoke fringed with crimson,
S carlet birds in mountains high.

Eleanor Harris (12) St John Fisher & Thomas More RC
High School

SEASONS

The lambs gambol in the fields nearby,
Birds can be seen high up in the sky.
Crocuses and daffodils burst into flower,
The sun shines bright with an occasional shower.
Everything seems to be bursting into bloom,
Spring is here and blossom fills the room.

It's warm and humid on a hot summer's day,
The ponds are alive with frogs today.
Flowers and their perfumes are all around,
Vegetables and fruits thrusting up from the ground,
Bees and wasps fly up in the air,
In summer even the birds their baths will share.

Red, gold and brown show their beautiful hues,
It's no time to feel any kind of blues.
For now is the time for collecting kindling wood,
A cooler season round the fire to be stood.
These are the times to be wearing warmer clothes,
At last autumn is upon us but in three months it goes.

The days are long and the nights are cold,
Glancing through the window the snow is white and bold.
The robin is here again with his breast so red,
The sheep are not on the hills but in their shed.
It is Jack Frost that is here,
Winter is his time of year.

Frances Later (12) St John Fisher & Thomas More
High School

193

BURNLEY FC

Come in my room and try to see,
which football team fascinates me.
It's not Man United, Leeds or Chelsea,
Yes, you've guessed it, Burnley FC.
I go on Saturdays, supporters and all,
Just to see players kicking a ball.
Parky our defender, out to stop,
Eyres and Robbo, willing to take a shot.
Beresford, well what a lovely bum,
That's nothing to do with it says my mum.
He has a job to do, keep the ball out the net,
Whether pitch is dry or if it's wet.
No excuses will Jimmy take,
If ball goes in the net he'll get earache.
So here's to the lads on the team,
Keep up the good work we think you're supreme.
God bless the refs great and small,
And for God's sake keep your eye on the ball.
We know there's mistakes in this game,
Make none with us or you'll go home lame.
Here's to Jimmy, well what a guy,
He keeps the team going with a 'tata pie.
At 90 pence we think they're nice,
But even better at half the price.
I like to get mine after the game,
At 50 pence, they're just the same.
Well till next week I'll finish here,
I'll leave you all with one last cheer,
Away the lads!

Karina Rawlinson (12) St John Fisher & Thomas More
High School

I AM BRUIN

One day as the show was about to begin,
people came from everywhere,
My master said out loud to me, 'Dance, bear dance.'
So I raised my dusty feet up off the ground,
And started to dance about the floor,
The children laughed out loud to see a great big dancing bear,
My master was kicking me, slapping me, telling me what to do,
He didn't care either, he just wanted money,
After the show I was breathless, thirsty and tired,
So I decided no more, I can't take the pain,
Late at night, I left with my chain wrapped around my neck,
I met another slave and we escaped together,
We went down to the sea and saw the silver path,
Everyone was coming towards us,
But we walked along the path,
The moonpath,
Out of sight,
Never coming back.

Claire Donnelly (12) St John Fisher & Thomas More
High School

NELLIE

There was once a dog called Nellie,
Who sat in a bowl full of jelly,
The jelly went *squish* and fell out of its dish,
And the dog landed flat on her belly.

Emma Bradshaw (12) St John Fisher & Thomas More RC
High School

SCHOOL'S OUT

Oooo yeah, school's out!

Screaming, shouting running round,
Wrestling each other to the ground.
Girls skipping and flirting with boys,
Whilst others sit and play with toys.
Teachers just can't keep control,
Kids just drive them up the wall.
Sticking spiders up their shirts,
And biting, Ow! That must hurt.
Older boys always play football,
While all the girls have a game of netball.
Some boys have a wrestling match
Whilst others play with the dog Patch.
Some girls have a running race,
And some like to play kiss-chase.
All the children have a ball
Until the head begins to call.
'Come on kids get home!
Or I'll have to take you to the phone,
And tell your parents what you've done,
They won't be pleased especially your mum!'
So all the children go home,
Poor teachers! You've gotta let them groan!

Danielle Wyld (11) St John Fisher & Thomas More
High School

CHRISTMAS

It's Christmas Eve and all is calm
The snow falls gently on the farm
Animals are sleeping in the hay
Soon it will be Christmas Day

The children are all safe and sound
In their beds with warmth around
The stockings lie empty at the end of the bed
'They'll soon be filled' their mother said

In the morning the children awake
'Please slow down for goodness sake'
Presents being opened with cries of joy
'Oh thank you mum for this lovely toy.'

Sally O'Regan (12) St John Fisher & Thomas More
High School

WHY?

I walked down the stairs with tears in my eyes,
Why had they told me so many lies,
I thought they liked me, I really did,
But now I know they think I'm a kid,
They only used me to make a joke,
It makes me sick, I could just choke,
For two years I was their dummy,
Now I have a sick feeling in my tummy,
Why did I let them run my life?
Why, oh why, oh why, oh why?

Laura Colvin (13) St John Fisher & Thomas More RC
High School

WAR

You're in the front line trenches,
You've got your life on the line,
They're breaking through all your defences,
And you're running out of time!

Your fear takes over,
You set off running back,
If you don't find any cover,
You'll get a bullet in your back!

The bangs are getting louder,
They're ringing in your ears,
You take your rifle in your hand,
And you wipe away your tears.

You're staring down the barrel,
Spying anything that flickers,
Your opposition's in your sight,
So you ease back on the trigger.

As the hammer makes the connection,
There comes a banging sound,
The bullet flies in his direction,
Then he falls to the ground.

The bombs stop for just a second,
You see him on the floor,
Every day our lives are threatened,
But all's fair in love and war!

Adam Grant (12) St John Fisher & Thomas More
High School

AUTUMN DAY

Dawn's just breaking, foggy and grey.
The wind is strong,
The air is cold.
It feels frosty and damp.

Autumn day leaves cover the ground,
Trees burst with fiery, golden colours.
Children playing in the leaves,
Looking for conkers from horsechestnut trees.

Evening comes, the roaring fire crackles and flickers.
Fireworks zoom into the sky,
Exploding like a fountain.
Then slowly disappearing into the night.

*Rebecca Villiers (11) St John Fisher & Thomas More RC
High School*

THE CHINESE QUEEN

Proud and tall, with a face so white,
Sapphires gleaming and diamonds bright,
Pointed nails, and staring eyes,
A face so cruel, but a mind so wise.

Silk and velvet robes she does wear
And a crown of jewels on her black hair.
Treasure chambers full of gold,
These all belong to the queen so old.

*Charlotte Bradshaw (12) St John Fisher & Thomas More
RC High School*

MY REFLECTION

I look in the water and what do I see
My own face staring at me

Then I look even closer and what do I see
The trees behind waving at me.

**Michael Bann (12) St John Fisher & Thomas More RC
High School**

ANIMALS OF THE FOREST

Elephants are so *big* and *grey*,
They sleep by night and play by day.
They wander around in the forest so deep,
Until they go back home to sleep.

The lion is the king of the beasts,
He hunts his prey and then he feasts
On deer, zebra, antelope or ox,
Sometimes rabbit, tiger or fox.

Zebras are striped, black and white,
Sometimes this helps them get out of sight.
When people come to hunt them down,
Whoever does this must be a clown!

Monkeys swing with their arms so long,
Dancing to the birds' sweet song.
When the dawn breaks through the night,
The monkeys swing out of sight.

**Vicky Real (12) St John Fisher & Thomas More RC
High School**

HUMOUR

Since time began
It's been man's aim
To overcome wrath
With the power of laugh
From mimics and mime
To gimmicks that rhyme
They're packing them in
For comedy time

Overcome problems
When listening to jokes.
Your time is up
That's all folks!
Cheerio.

Joey-Lee Deehan (12) St John Fisher & Thomas More RC
High School

THE POLAR BEAR'S PREY

In a mysterious far land of snow and ice
Hides a white bleak coat of darkness
Its face is like a teddy bear
Cute but dangerous
With its eyes like black spears
It looks for its prey
And with Its razor sharp teeth
It eats it alive.

Sharron Connor (13) St John Fisher & Thomas More RC
High School

CATS

Life can be slow or life can be fast,
Sometimes gentle, sometimes vast.
Some are black and some are white,
There's lots of different cats I like.

Kittens are probably the best I like,
Sometimes friendly, sometimes they bite.
Learning the tricks of later life,
Of how to stalk and get into strife.

Cats are lazy, they like to sleep,
They sleep long and they sleep deep.
Whey they awake, they are ready for food,
Which always puts them in a rather good mood.

Now it's time to catch their prey,
Which they always do at the end of the day.
They bring mice, which are not very nice,
Then lick them up like sugar and spice.

Louise Coates (12) St John Fisher & Thomas More RC
High School

REFLECTIONS

Trees like silk in the air whisking away
Bushes wafting away like leaves flying in the air
Children with their parents floating like paper
And bridges being suspended by the water front

Cars like cotton drifting slowly
Boats like rubber bending softly
The sun shining up like a blaze of fire
And birds flying upside down.

Steven Fenwick (12) St John Fisher & Thomas More RC
High School

202

THE MERMAID

What would it feel like to be a mermaid?
Gliding in the waters so blue,
Dodging the fish and the waving coral,
Beneath the waters so deep.

Amanda Brennan (12) St John Fisher & Thomas More RC
High School

THE SWORD FIGHT

Black drew his sword
White cautiously drew his
Black struck the first blow
White tumbled to the ground
Black sliced his sword into the air
Suddenly White jumped to his feet
He struck back at Black, white liquid flowed out of Black's leg
Black fell to the ground and cried out
Has Black been defeated?
With one great effort, Black got up
Black struck a mighty blow
White fell to the ground heavily
He didn't get up, he just stayed on the floor
White had lost!
Black had won!

Theresa Bean (12) St John Fisher & Thomas More RC
High School

I AM BRUIN

As I heard the master yell, 'To the ground'
I tumbled to the floor,
As feeling great pain,
I heard the crowd shouting, 'More! More! More!'

The master rattled his chains
And shouted, 'To your feet'
I scrambled up
And felt the blazing, burning, flaming heat.

I heard the children laugh and scream,
They'd probably never seen so much fun,
But for me, I've never been in so much agony,
I wish I could just run and run and run.

Stephanie Briggs (12) St John Fisher & Thomas More RC
High School

THE POLAR BEAR

A polar bear who couldn't spell
Sat thinking in the snow
I wish I could tell
If snow or skno is right
As he sat there thinking
A hunter came up and shot him
So the polar bear will never know.

Heather Morrison (12) St John Fisher & Thomas More RC
High School

I AM BRUIN

Misery, pain, torment, day after day.
I walk this cage, my home for the past four years.
I cannot run,
I cannot stand high on my two powerful hind legs.

I yearn to smell the pine leaves and
Roll in the crisp white glistening snow of my homeland.
Instead I wear a heavy metal rusty chain
Which rubs my neck until it bleeds.
I dance and march in the street.
Sounds all around frighten me.

I sweat in the heat of the midday sun.
I thirst from the dust of the dirty roads.
I am whipped when I don't perform well.

I eat old dead meat which gives me no pleasure.
I didn't chase it.
I didn't kill it.
I didn't bring it triumphantly home to my family.
Misery, pain, torment, day after day.

Matthew Perry (12) St John Fisher & Thomas More RC
High School

SUMMER

Summer, when every leaf is on its tree
When a robin's not a beggar
A field full of flowers
With just a slight breeze
When ladybirds arrive.

Martin Eyre (11) St John Fisher & Thomas More RC
High School

ADDICTION

I have an addiction,
I'm ashamed to say,
It's got so bad now,
It's a few times a day.

There's dark and there's light,
There's nutty and white,
There's soft and there's creamy,
It makes me all dreamy.

It's given by lovers,
To show that they care,
If you go into a shop,
It will always be there.

I love it, I love it!
I always want more,
You've guessed it - you're right!
It's chocolate I adore.

Emily Armas (12) St John Fisher & Thomas More RC
High School

THE BIG BEAR

In the woods,
Under the tree,
There is a big bear.
He is ready to give you a scare.

If you go into the woods tonight,
He will give you a nasty fright.
Then if you try to run away,
He will get you another day.

Damien Phillips (11) St John Fisher & Thomas More RC
High School

IN MY HOT BATH

In my hot bath
I see a shuttlecraft
With a man in a suit
Standing upside down
The man is drowning
The shuttlecraft is sinking
And all I can see is double

Two shuttlecrafts
And two men
I put my hands in the water,
The waves are going up and down
The man's heart is pounding
And then one shuttlecraft disappears
And when the waves stop.
Two shuttlecrafts come back.

Samantha Butterworth (12) St John Fisher & Thomas More
RC High School

NIGHT POND

The still blue pond
when it's almost dark
like a looking glass
in the middle of the park.

The stars in the sky
and the bright full moon
reflects on the water
on this evening in June.

The lamp by the pond
with its orange light
like an Olympic torch
burning so bright.

Adrian Iannazzo (12) St John Fisher & Thomas More RC
High School

SPRING

Spring, spring,
Is a wonderful thing.
The flowers bloom
And the birds do sing.
The lambs are born
And the sheep are shorn.
Spring, spring
Is a wonderful thing.

Spring, spring,
Is a wonderful thing.
The days turn long
And the birds sing their song.
The buds return on the trees,
For the world and its enchanting scenes.
Spring, spring,
Is a wonderful thing.

Joanne Smith (12) St John Fisher & Thomas More RC
High School

THE MOUSE

Oh little mouse you are so small
Unlike the trees who are so tall
You romp about and play all day
And then at night lay in the hay
You stare at the moon so big and bright
And watch for the owls who swoop and bite
And when day breaks
You have to hide
For cats are roaming
Far and wide

Lisa McDermott (12) St John Fisher & Thomas More RC
High School

208

I AM BRUIN

I'm locked up in a cage
The sun is blazing on my back
The chains on my feet dig into my leg
I'm lonesome and dejected
No-one wants me

The days are hot
The nights are breathless
My feet are dusty
I'm hungry and thirsty
I'm scared

I'm homesick and lonesome
I want to go home
Where I can live and roam alone.

Daniel Pitman (12) St John Fisher & Thomas More RC
High School

THE DEADLY CROC

This poisonous frog.
This deadly croc,
With jaws of steel!
It would kill the poor frog.
However the frog can bite back!
Still inside the croc's mouth,
It could still use its poison to kill it.
I wonder what happened?
Was it just as I thought,
Did the frog get away?
Or is it in the croc's throat?

Philip Atkinson (12) St John Fisher & Thomas More RC
High School

'WANNA COME TO MY HOUSE?'

My mum says I can't.
I've got loads of homework.
I've got to go shopping.
My dad says I'm grounded.
My cat's just died.
My dog is sick.
I'm going to my great aunt's.
I've got French relations visiting.
The house has been burgled.
Mum's getting me a rabbit.
I've got to go to the dentist.
In other words *'No!'*

Adam Palmer (12) St John Fisher & Thomas More RC
                                              High School

A PUPPY

I used to have a puppy,
Who loved to have a hug,
And sometimes a tug.

He loved to chase cats
But mostly lay on the mats.

He curled up on his bed
But best of all on uncle Ted.

When someone called he barked
And ran out in the dark
A long tail and puffy feet
He really was very sweet.

Angela Wallwork (12) St John Fisher & Thomas More RC
                                                 High School

HURRICANE

Hurricanes are very powerful
They knock down trees like pins on a bowling set.
It's like a huge person blowing.

Crunching leaves whilst people flee.
Screaming whilst they run,
Buildings swaying side to side.

Trees hitting cars and buildings
Cars up in the air
Including a little boy.

Oil drums rolled around like snooker balls.
Rivers broke their banks and flooded houses.
The church steeple was blown to the ground.

Ships tossed and sank in the rough seas.
Also lightning hit a pylon
Trees laid on the floor.

Then the eye of the storm was overhead.

Richard Thornton (11) St John Fisher & Thomas More RC
High School

MY CAT

Mysterious is what you are
Your long sleek body going far
Coming and going, in and out
All the time you run about
The time has come to seek you out.

Emma Dundon (12) St John Fisher & Thomas More RC
High School

SEASONS

Spring comes and brings the rain,
Baby lambs, calves and foals again.

Summer comes and brings the flowers,
Greens the trees and lengthens the hours.

Autumn comes and strips the trees
And birds start to fly away for winter.

Winter comes and freezes everything,
Christmas comes, we all get presents.
The birds have flown away for winter.

Emma-Louise Goddard (11) St John Fisher & Thomas More
RC High School

A CAT'S POINT OF VIEW

Down with the dog!
Down with his bone!
Down with his owner!
Moan! Moan! Moan!

Down with his fleas!
Down with his *woof!*
Down with his *grrr!*
Huff! Huff! Huff!

Down with his collar!
Down with man's best friend!
Down with it all!
End! End! End!

James Tanner (12) St John Fisher & Thomas More RC
High School

A HEALING SPELL

Heal, heal, heal my finger
Hurry up, do not linger
I cannot use it anymore
Because it is so very sore
Bark of a log
A whisker of a dog
A cat's tail
A tooth of a whale
A wing of a bat
That's enough of that
Stir it all up
And put it in a cup
Now swallow it down
Ugh! It makes me frown
Now my finger is all well
I can bottle this to sell.

Victoria Ormerod (11) St John Fisher & Thomas More
RC High School

DARN MY DOG

Darn my dog taking her walks!
Darn my dog's horrible smell!
Darn my dog sleeping on my bed!
Dead! Dead! Dead!
Darn my dog's sloppy food!
Darn my dog's smelly chew!
Darn my dog's dead brain!
Pain! Pain! Pain!
Darn my dog's horrible tail!
Darn my dog's bow on its bum!
Darn my dog's smelly breath!
Death! Death! Death!

Simon Robert Hewitt (12) St John Fisher & John More RC
High School

THE EVERGREEN TREE

The morning that summer came
The willow tree howled with delight
'What about the evergreen tree?'
'Oh!' said I, 'she'll be alright!'

'What if she hurts herself?
What if she cuts her toes?'
'Oh! That doesn't matter
As long as she still grows!'

'Oh dear, when will it be winter?'
'Not until autumn has passed!'
'When will that be? Is it soon?'
'No! Days don't go very fast.'

Nicola McCaigue (11) St John Fisher & Thomas More RC
High School

HURRICANE

Hurricane a cloud of dust,
Went whistling through a darkened wood.
It tramples on all trees green,
Howling rumbling in terrifying mood,
Scaring animals great and small,
Frightening birds out of trees so tall.
Rushing hissing blowing past.
Whirling strong whirling fast.
Nothing escapes this terrible storm.
Everything suffers everything's harmed.
Hurricanes are so frightening
When whistling through a darkened wood.

Beki Wilkinson (12) St John Fisher & Thomas More RC
High School

CHRISTMAS TIME

Christmas is a happy time
Mums and dads wine and dine.
Children sing so happy and free
Gathered round the Christmas tree.

Santa comes through snow and ice
Bringing things sweet and nice.
Rudolf with his nose so red
Wishes he was back in bed.
Snug and warm eating hay
Waiting until the next Christmas day.

Carol singers knock on doors
The Christmas spirit stops all wars.
Santa's sleigh is being driven
Presents being given.
Santa's reindeers' hooves
Stamping on people's roofs.
People go to midnight mass
While Santa travels first class.

Thomas Morrison (11) St John Fisher & Thomas More RC
High School

PEPPER

Pepper is my guinea pig,
When she is hungry she does a jig,
She is fairly old about seven,
So she soon might be going up to heaven.
She's black and white with a bit of brown
And has a little fluffy crown,
She is very big and fat
And scares the next door neighbour's cat.

Rachael Schofield (12) St John Fisher & Thomas More RC
High School

DEATH

When I think about life after death
I get a cold chill down my spine.
I don't like the thought of dying
But people die all the time.

When my parents die
I don't know what I'll do -
Maybe my skin will turn blue
I'll look like a Martian, but I don't care
All I'll really want is love and a teddy bear!

Who wants to live forever?
I keep hearing people say,
Who wants to live forever?
But people die everyday.

Maria Mendola (13) St John Fisher & Thomas More RC
High School

APRIL

April was standing there,
Standing in the fresh country air,
I tied her to the stable door,
As I swept the stable floor.
Her chestnut coat gleamed in the light,
Her lovely brown eyes were sparkling bright,
I brushed her coat with her tack,
For we were riding to the church and back.

Sandra Gwinnett (12) St John Fisher & Thomas More RC
High School

DUSK

Dusk!
It was silent over the barracks
Except for the odd flutter of leathery wings
As bats hunted down their prey.

The wail of the alarm
Broke the silence
Soldiers fumbled as they quickly dressed
Tripping and stumbling over empty
Beer cans from last night's party.

There wasn't a sound as they all
Stepped outside into the trenches,
Trying to keep calm under enemy fire.

The scout party
Set off into the moonlight
Quiet as mice,
Except for the soft squelching sound
Coming from the muddy earth.

Unlucky for them they walked straight
Into a minefield
Their bloodstained clothes
Littered the ground
(What a way to go)

**Stephen Wademan (12) St John Fisher & Thomas More RC
High School**

217

KILLER WHALES

Kind and gentle are the waves
Icy cold the water stays,
Little whales and big ones too
Lunge around the waters blue
Every mile they swim with ease
Round the ocean swim as they please.
Why, so freely they do swim
How I wonder if they will win
As the fishermen start the fight
Look! They swim with all their might
Easily they swim away
Silently they go to play!

Victoria Hargreaves (13) St John Fisher & Thomas More RC
High School

218

WHY DID I LEAVE HOME?

I'm hungry, I'm thirsty
In the damp, cold forest I lay,
Where no-one can eat me and
No-one can kill me
So here I will stay.

I'm a hamster, I'm fluffy,
I'm hairy, I'm lonely,
I'm hungry, I'm thirsty,
If only . . .

Why did I leave home?
I ask myself in grief
Why didn't I stop there?
I don't want to be a thief.

To steal my food
Under heaven's blue dome
Where I could have everything
If I stayed at home.

Gemma McCaigue (12) St John Fisher & Thomas More RC
High School

HENRY VIII

Give me a divorce!
Give me a son!
Give me a new wife!
Now! Now! Now!
Give me an axe!
Give me a block!
Give me a mask!
Chop! Chop! Chop!
Give me Jane!
Give me Joy!
Give me an heir!
Boy! Boy! Boy!

Anna Walsh (12) St John Fisher & Thomas More RC
                                        High School

DOWN

Down with jobs
Down with rules
Down with 'Will you tidy your room?'
Fools! Fools! Fools!

Down with school
Down with snoring
Down with homework
Boring! Boring! Boring!

Down with sport
Down with pies
What am I saying - All
Lies! Lies! Lies!

Stephen James Kennedy (12) St John Fisher & Thomas More
                                        RC High School

AUTUMN

This way that way
Swirling twirling twisting
Turning to the
Ground.
Stamp!
Stamp!
Crickle crackle
Go leaves on the
Ground.
Collecting twigs and wood
From the woodland floor,
For bonfires on
Bonfire night
For fireworks
That go whoosh! Bang!
In the night.
The smoky smell
Makes you
Cough and
Choke
Eyes water more and more.

Sally Marshall (11) St John Fisher & Thomas More RC
High School

GRAVEYARD GHOST

I walked through the graveyard,
A short cut home from school,
And there it was, it was a ghoul,
My head filled with fright,
The day had turned to night,
It glanced, I stared,
I knew I was scared,
My hair stood on end,
I could not defend,
I ran and I screamed,
I woke up it was a dream.

Charlotte Hind (11) St John Fisher & Thomas More RC
High School

MONKEY

A little monkey short and cute,
With his box head and evil eyes,
So furry, fluffy and small,
Jumping from tree to tree.
It's spooky in a sort of way
For he has a tube nose and a box head
I think he is ugly and fat
But also cute.
It's really weird to explain
He is frizzy and furry
But those eyes are really evil
Evil, evil, eyes!

Stephanie Sharples (12) St John Fisher & Thomas More RC
High School

DEATH TO THE SISTER

Death to the sister!
Death to her schemes!
Death to her rotten ways!
Scream? Scream? Scream?

Death to her friends!
Death to her life!
Death to her being my sister!
Why! Why! Why!

Death to her 'That's mine!'
Death to her 'I'm going first!'
Death to her 'I'm older than you!'
Curse! Curse! Curse!

Lisa Robinson (12) St John Fisher & Thomas More RC
High School

THE HURRICANE

The hurricane goes round and round,
sweeping things off the ground,
it goes as fast as a car
and the people scream and run very far.

People are dying
children are crying
the leaves are moving
and sweeping and leaping
up and down they blow.

Lauren Haigh (11) St John Fisher & Thomas More RC
High School

MONSTERS

When I was young
There was a monster under my bed
It once was alive but now it's dead.
It used to roam around at night.
And it used to give me a fright
I thought it was under my sister's bed.
It was under my mum and dad's bed too
Under the bath, the table and the sofa.

It shuffled around in cupboards
It crept past my door on creaking floorboards.
I ran up the ladders to my bed
Because the monster was growling behind me.

There was once a monster under my bed
It once was alive but now it's dead!

*Andrew Waterhouse (11) St John Fisher & Thomas More RC
High School*

THE MOUNTAIN RIVERS

River fast
river slow
Running on the mountain floor
When it stops
Where it goes
On the river
No-one knows.

*Michael Greenwood (13) St John Fisher & Thomas More RC
High School*

REFLECTIONS OF ME

Reflections, reflections,
Reflections of me.
I looked in the mirror,
What did I see?
A reflection of me.

Reflections, reflections,
Reflections of me.
I see me in a rain puddle
I see me as a shadow
Tall and thin wearing black, like a widow.

Reflections, reflections,
Reflections of me
I see me in a river bank
Colourful; wonderful
Colours of me.
Pink, brown shades of blue
Just like a butterfly.

Rebecca Owen (12) St John Fisher & Thomas More RC
High School

WHAT IS A POEM?

What is a poem?
A poem is words,
A poem rhymes
It's about trees, flowers and birds.

A poem can be anything
About horror, people and places.
Just make sure it fits
And don't leave any spaces.

A poem can have lots of verses,
Also punctuation.
It can have a rhythm
And even alliteration.

Humorous poems are very good,
And don't make me pout,
Serious poems make me sad
I wonder what my next poem will be about!

Katherine Dickinson (13) St John Fisher & Thomas More RC
High School

THE FLUTTERING REFLECTION

A   flickering   side   side
  butterfly   from   to
Across a fluttering river
A shallow movement

         To
And fro
         To
And fro

The reflection turns to darkness
As the butterfly breaks the skin of the water

        Up   Up
Bobbing   and   and
              down   down
And reaches
        Land.

Jon Green (12) St John Fisher & Thomas More RC
High School

227

CONKERS

Conkers, conkers everywhere
on the trees and in my hair,
there's just one conker it's the best
it has beaten all the rest.

I like the look of a conker
it is dark or light brown,
whenever I see a conker
it is dangling down.

The rule of the game conkers
is to smash the other one's first,
if you hit it hard enough
the other may burst.

I like the game conkers
it's a new experience to me,
whenever I smash a conker
everyone is proud of me.

Alistair Eccles (12) St John Fisher & Thomas More RC
High School

PLANET EARTH

Planet earth, my home, my place,
Just a small speck in a sea of space.
Planet earth, are you just
Floating by a cloud of dust,
A tiny globe about to bust,
A piece of metal bound to rust,
A block of matter in a mindless void,
A lonely spaceship, a large asteroid?

Do you care, have you a part?
In the deepest emotions of my own heart
Tender with breezes, caressing and whole,
Alive with music, haunting my soul,
Planet earth, gentle and blue,
With all my heart,
I love you.

Kate Sophia Targett (12) St John Fisher & Thomas More RC High School

FEELINGS

Guile can make the weakest mighty
And the powerful crumble
It can wreck lives and break hearts
Once deceived people do not trust
Love becomes anger happiness becomes hate
Guile possesses minds and turns them evil
Sadness drains life from a soul
Your heart is full of nothing but a void
To you there is no difference between life and death
Sadness creates a false guilt
Burdens are amplified when you feel blue
When I feel sad the reason for living escapes me
When you are in love your soul is as high as a kite
Nothing could weigh your soul down
No burden is too great
No problem is too big
A dream is like another world
A reality where dreams come true
It is a place where you may lead a different life
It's a world far greater than our own.
Dreams are real.

Bradley Whitehead (12) Saddleworth School

CONSTIPATION

I sit on the loo and try and try,
My eyes begin to water and I start to cry.
I clench my teeth and punch the walls,
I wish I'd finished the bowl of bran balls.
I heave and I ho but it won't come out,
So I go red in the face and start to shout:
'Oh why am I landed with this fate worse than death?
I'd rather have zits or steaming bad breath.'

Mother quick go down the shop.
And get me a remedy that'll make these pains stop.
Branflakes, branballs, fibre as well,
Maybe these things can get me out of this hell.

I've been here now for two hours or more,
There's a queue outside banging on the door.
Just don't rush me now it's a delicate job,
It's damn hard trying to get out this dirty great bob.
Ticking away, two hours already gone,
It's like giving birth to a water melon.
Yes, it's out I sigh with relief,
I wipe away the mess and pull up my briefs.
Open the door and dance with joy,
Mum pats me on the head and says, 'Who's a clever boy?'

Tom Barrow (13) Saddleworth School

MY BROTHER

My brother is a little lad,
Short and stout but rather sad.
He's one of those retiring folk,
Who does not laugh, does not joke.
He lives a sort of backwards life,
Full of sorrow, full of strife.

He sits in his room day after day,
And sometimes he, to my dismay
Scoffs my sweets and I shout 'Hey
Get off you little scheming thief
Or I'll fill your life full of grief.'
He looks at me, laughs and jeers,
Suddenly his eyes fill with tears.
For he is hanging upside down,
Suspended in his dressing gown,
He screams let me down or I'll tell on you,
I said shut up you little pooh.

After five minutes, with a frown,
I set him back onto the ground,
I went out and down the stairs,
He gave me one of those funny glares.
I decided not to retaliate,
For I was tired, and it was getting late.
The time has come, it's time for bed,
My eyelids feel like lumps of lead.
This is now my penultimate line,
Auf Wiedersehen, chow, until next time.

Tom Sweet (14) Saddleworth School

THE GOLDFISH

Swimming round in the shimmering water,
The fish glides gracefully along.
Its slimy wet body shines
Like gold.

Flakes float over the water surface.
The fish bobs up and
Down grabbing the food
And sucking it into its mouth.
Its fins go down as it swims
Frantically.

When sleeping the goldfish's
Blood shot eyes stay wide open.
As it floats in the water not
At the top not at the bottom
But in between.
Only waking at the sound of
Food being dropped in the water.

Karen Nicholls (12) Saddleworth School

THE KESTREL

The kestrel flew across the sky,
Looking for defenceless prey.
Scanning the ground with piercing eyes,
Like a radar looking for other crafts.

Dagger beak, glinting in the sun,
Sounding out an icy cry.
Claws poised ready, ready to snatch,
A victim preparing to die.

As fast as a cheetah,
The silent descent.
The fieldmouse collapses in fright,
His plight was in vain.

Dug into flesh, the bloodstained talons,
Lifting the limp lifeless rag.
Gripping tightly squeezing out life,
Like a dripping tap.

Victoria Stothard (12) Saddleworth School

STARVATION

The children of Ethiopia
Don't have food to eat
They don't have water to drink
Not a computer, or games to play
Or half the things you think.

These children don't have houses,
No avenue or street
They just wander around helplessly
And thirsty in the heat.

Starvation is a horrible word
It should have no meaning in this world
It brings tears to my eyes
So next time, think of those starving
Before you eat your pies.

Katie Bradley (14) Saddleworth School

A POEM ABOUT DETENTION

I walked into maths today
And to my utmost dismay,
I don't know why it come this way
But I would have not wanted to stay.

I sat down at my desk,
Decided I would be a pest,
He always picks on me
Why doesn't he ever see.

A girl by me was chewing gum
At the same time sucking her thumb
She spat the chewing gum so far,
It hit the teacher
And stuck in his hair.

He turned around, and looked at me,
He was the colour of a pea,
I don't think he did really care,
Who threw the gum into his hair.

He seemed to be glancing
Round to see,
Who was looking the most guilty,
Guess who looked so calm and witty.

I looked at him and began to laugh
He looked as though he was on the warpath
I don't believe I still could smile
This detention would be for a while.

'An hour, for you, you little twit,'
Oh no I don't believe it
I didn't even do the deed,
But now I've taken all the speed.

Leah Moore (14) Saddleworth School

THE VAMPIRE

The air was dark, dank, full of gloom,
The vampire was sleeping alone in her tomb.
When the moon was full, she creaked upon the lid,
And this is the terrible thing that she did.

She stalked the night with a devilish grin,
Nobody knowing the cunning within.
She snook to the hospital, she really was nasty,
Her idea was terrible really quite ghastly!

She prowled to the Royal, just round the corner,
Hoping her vampire friends wouldn't scorn her.
She entered the hospital, passed ward four,
Checking behind her, she opened the door.

The room she intruded really was smelly,
She stopped, then continued, it was going to fill her belly,
The vampire sucked from the tubing, until it ran thick,
After a while, the oozing blood made her quite sick.

She lay on the floor clutching her stomach,
this vampire was greedy, she'd had really too much.
So she slept near the blood bank, just on the ground,
In the light of the morning, here dead, she was found.

Jessica Davies (13) Saddleworth School

DEATH OF A DINOSAUR

A dinosaur wandering lonely as
The rain drumming off his scaly hide,
He slowly treads past,
The bleached white bones,
Of creatures once his kith and kin.
The cold chill of the dawning Ice Age,
Gradually pervades his sluggish body,
He slows, to an almost standstill,
Then halts by the carcass of his father,
He sinks to the floor, and on his knees,
Shakes his head but cannot clear it,
Cannot rise, and so lies still,
And the pounding of his great heart
Lessens, grows quieter, and then stops.
The chill of the Ice Age has begun.

Many more will rise and fall,
Wax and wane, but all in vain,
Shall tread the path their fathers trod,
And fall the way their fathers fell.
Throughout the aeons of evolution,
Many have risen, all have fallen,
No more can man expect to grasp,
Reptiles, dinos, finally man,
On this earth for a bare three million,
Trivial feeble civilisations,
Who now hold the world in power,
Held in power by great machines,
Mankind may rise, but come what may,
Man will fall, and die, like a whisper.

Hugh Caffrey (14) Saddleworth School

ABORTION

Mummy, mummy, I'm here inside
I can't wait until I'm out alive.
What will I hear? What will I see?
Mummy, tell me where I'm going to be?

Quite a long time yet,
A month, Or a year?
No! About 8 months
I can't wait to appear.

Will it be morning
Or will it be night?
Will it be dark
Or will it be light?
Mummy goodnight.

Mummy, it's morning,
But where are we going?
Mummy it's cold
It must be snowing.

It's getting colder
I can hardly see
Mummy help,
What's happening to me?

I'm here in your dreams mum,
Talking to you.
Mummy I love you
Tell daddy I love him too.

Marisa Hill (14) Saddleworth School

EXCOMMUNICATION

George was a friendly man,
  a funny man,
  a happy man.

George lived in a house,
  in a street,
  in a town.
But now he lives in the gutters.

George had a family, a wife,
     a son,
     a daughter.

But now they're dead.

George had a car accident,
   a broken rib,
   a six year sentence
But now he's free.

George has freedom,
  no money,
  no house,
  no family,
  just sadness,
  a guilty conscience
  and freedom!

Daniel Parkes (14) Saddleworth School

ARMY

The blasting of guns
The bombs dropping
The screams of pain
People dying
Freedom is far, far away
Platoons in the bushes
Guns at the ready
Bombs in the hand
The approach of Death
Grown men terrified
Now thinking back to when they joined
thinking about their families at home
They want to get out
The screams
The pain
Dead friends
The cry of pain
It's terrifying
No-one escapes the face of Death
They run
Too scared to shoot
When finally they fail
They wanted Glory
But found pain
Just pain.

Luke Higgins (12) The Radclyffe School

241

THE FOX HUNT

A murderer in a blood red coat,
Mounts his horse, lets loose his hounds,
Joins a group of other men,
Who listen to the awful sounds,
Of barking dogs who roughly chase,
A panting, panicked, frightened fox,
A look of terror on its face.
Running over fields and hills,
The fox's vision blurred with fear,
It stumbles through the jagged grass,
And picks up speed as the hounds draw near.
It's breathing fast and hard and deep,
The fox's heart thumps in its chest,
Its legs feel like they're made of lead,
The fox just wants to sleep, to rest.
The murderer watches from his horse,
And chuckles at the fox's fright,
He gallops through a muddy stream,
On his horse with hair as black as night.
And as the fox's legs give way
And it takes one final, painful fall,
the murderer's one and only thought,
Is of another trophy for his wall.

Sarah Hilton (13) The Radclyffe School

WHEN THE DAY COMES

When the day comes,
The sky will turn black,
And the psychics will not be amused,
Buildings will crumble and fall,
The people running, bemused.

The underground fall outs are opened,
Their motto is first come, first served,
But for the people who did not get in
Their screams from the bunkers aren't heard.

The last TV broadcast goes out on the air,
The newsreader's final report.
The person who pushed the button of death,
Will end up in Heaven's High Court.

So the world will go into melt down,
The Army, despite tanks and guns,
Will not stop the big bomb from dropping
The day that our doomsday comes.

Timothy Drane (14) The Radclyffe School

CRICKET

Silence as the bowler shines
the ball.

The tension mounts as he
starts to pace.

Long, fast bowler thundering
down the crease.

Swings his arm,
the ball's on fire.

The fielder jumps higher

Out! The batsman's a crier!

Aslam Amin (12) The Radclyffe School

THE SPACE MAN

I've travelled from far, from light years away,
Forever I've travelled until this day.
I come with fear, I come with dread,
Is what the peculiar space man said.

I've come not to ruin but study your earth,
to see the miracle of creation give birth,
But now I am here, there's nothing to see,
No singing of bird, no buzzing of bee.

Here is my story, I do hope you'll listen,
The story of why the earth does not glisten,
It happened far back, I was just a boy,
There's now no more singing, there's now no more joy.

Men did argue and quarrel together,
Now the earth is a wasteland for ever.
They used to have wars with bomb after bomb,
With guns and strange weapons, it goes on and on.

They kept on improving, there was always tomorrow,
Not wanting to give, but always to borrow.
They wanted more money and new things to buy,
But why work for money for tomorrow we die.

The world was polluted, the atmosphere dying,
Their life was a struggle, they just went on sighing,
But then in one war was a nuclear bomb,
The men they did use it, the world doesn't go on.

David Lepton Pulo (13) The Radclyffe School

IMAGE OF WAR

I was promoted to Sergeant Major today,
It's a better position with much better pay.
The lads in the Squadron say I'm in for it now,
I'll have to start killing, I'd better learn how.

But I'm not afraid, for I know what's in store,
There'll be hand grenades, bombs, tanks, planes galore.
I'll stand at the front with a target in sight,
My gun will be raised, I'll be ready to fight.

The war has begun, bullets fly through the sky,
I'm here with the lads, I'm here willing to die.
We'll travel through desert sun, cold winds and sleet,
And stand on dead bodies that lie at our feet.

The war it has ended, a year has now gone,
I remember my thoughts when the war had begun.
The town's buildings lie round me, broken up on the ground,
Over poor helpless people who'll never be found.

I left my position as Sergeant Major today,
That once better job with its thousand pound pay.
I gave in my gun, I don't fight anymore,
As there's no need for violence, there's no need for war.

Lynette Greenwood (14) The Radclyffe School

THE LION

He prowls through the jungle,
Searching for prey,
The sound of a motor
Sends him scampering away.

He runs through the jungle,
Having some fun,
'Got him!' Shouts the hunter,
Bang goes his gun.

He can't hunt anymore,
He has no more fun,
No need to fear,
The sound of a gun.

His fur on display,
In the shopping precinct
The last one they'll own,
The lion's extinct.

Joanne Smith (14) The Radclyffe School

SEASONS

Spring, cool calm and collective,
Budding flowers bloom beautifully in fields,
lambs linger, new born, fresh from birth,
Birds return from winter sun, into the trees,
Newly bloomed, with leaves a new born green.

Summer, subsides into a warm haven of love,
The sun rises in the morn and sets at noon,
Giving a beautiful picture to the world, as the orange blends with the
red,
This gives an unimagined beauty to the world.

Autumn, comes along with the leaves falling to the ground,
The new born green leaves turn to a luscious red, yellow and brown,
The cold, windy, rain beats down on the ground, giving beautiful
sounds from trees,
As the year goes on the nights set in early with
The dark taking control of the cold day.

Winter comes and goes with snow settling softly on the ground,
Christmas trees lit with lanterns, tinsel and decorations,
The snowman stands in the yard, with a coal and a carrot for a face,
Sacks sit on the fireplace with presents round, the place decorated
with a feeling of love around,
Then so the year closes and the next new year
Opens for brand new tidings.

Stephen Astin (14) Walton High School

KILLING TIME

The killing fields are open
So enter all the punters.
Fill yourselves with beer and spirits
Then turn into hunters.

Pay your fee to cause some pain,
Then enjoy their sadness.
Laugh and joke, load your gun
In a ridicule of madness.

Don't let them run and get away
Shoot them with your gun.
And if you miss then try again
Don't let it spoil your fun.

When your so called sport is over,
Make sure you're feeling good.
Don't let yourself feel guilty
For the suffering and blood.

Why don't you take up sailing?
At least you'll sail on water.
Nowhere near the hunting ground
Which caused the pain and slaughter.

Cheryl Howarth (13) Walton High School

OUR POLLUTED CANAL

Plastic bags, rusty bikes,
No more fish, no more pike.

Plastic bottles, broken door,
Our canal looks very poor.

Floorboards from last year's floor,
Pollution cannot ask for more.

Ragged clothes, pieces of wood,
Our canal looks bad, not good.

Old prams, pieces of glass,
All the rubbish is in a mass.

Bits and bobs, my old mask,
Just trying to clean it is a task.

So when you throw rubbish think back to these days,
That rubbish you dump is dangerous in ways.
Rubbish hurts animals, even birds,
So think of this poem and remember these words.
Rubbish, rubbish, everywhere,
Pollution is in the air.

Gemma Doodson (12) Wardle High School

PRISONER

I'm so cold and so hungry,
When will it end.
The anger and the hatred
I plot my revenge.
The fear and the sadness
It's getting me down.
All the guards walking around,
They make me frown.
I'm bored and I'm homesick,
Let me break free.
I've got no life now,
I'm just a misery.
I feel cramped and there's lack of privacy,
Apart from that I miss my family and I'm lonely.
I'm cold and I'm hungry,
Oh please let it end,
All the anger and hatred
I still plot my revenge.

Kirsty Plumb (11) Wardle High School

FRIENDS

I thought she was my friend,
I must be wrong,
Why won't she play with me?
Is my nose that long?

Who else can I play with?
I have no more friends
Please be my friend Angie,
And let's make amends.

Who else can I talk to?
Laura, maybe Joan,
No, they don't like me
So I'm going to be on my own.

Will someone please play with me
And be my best friend?
No-one will beat Angie
And my heart will never mend.

Angie, is my friend now,
It's like we never split up
She's coming over this weekend
To play with my new pup.

Charlotte Wilkin (11) Wardle High School

JOSEPH BALIKCI POEM

I feel as though everything I have
Has been taken from me,
My wonderful Mrs Balikci
And children have gone.
Including the one and only son,
And my two daughters also
I will always miss them all
I used to kiss them all
Goodnight.
They never used to fight,
They never used to whine
They were always friends,
Oh, how I miss them now.
And I always have.
I really want to see them
For real.
Instead of these tattered pictures
From my pocket,
All scrumpled and rumpled
Oh how I wish to see them.

Sarah Dean (11) Wardle High School

THE BOMB

In the shelter, we're on our own
There's three of us, me, mum and Joan.
We hear a plane it stops, no sound.
Deadly silence is all around.
I feel no fear, just anger and hate
That Hitler throws bombs at such a rate.
My mum is scared, I see her eyes
She tries to hide it with a sigh.
I am nine, well going on ten
I'll never see my dad again.
He went away an age ago
He was shot, mum told me so
I miss him lots, he was such fun
He would never harm anyone
We hear a whistle, then a bang
There goes the house of old Miss Crang
My mother cries and so does Joan
There's three of us, we're on our own.

Samantha Powers (12) Wardle High School

AIR RAID

It was cold dark and wet, I was stuck underground
I was very frightened, would I be found?
The bomb had landed just outside,
Everything had fallen in trapping me inside.
I needed help was there anyone about?
My chance of rescue was to shout and shout.
I heard a voice much later on.
I had been very lucky it was my friend John
He buried down through bricks and rubble,
He rescued me and got me out of trouble.

Helen Bollington (12) Wardle High School

TRAPPED

Here I am under this battered old door
I cannot see the light anymore
The sounds of bangs and sirens fill my head
Please God, let me not be dead
Underneath this blown up Anderson shelter.

I can hear our friend above the din
The people shake their heads and give in
There's a sound of someone digging at the rubble
It is joined by others taking the trouble
To get us out of this Anderson shelter.

Walking along beside our heroic friend
We know who we can always depend on
We talk about our lucky escape
From underneath that Anderson shelter.

Jane Edmondson (11) Wardle High School

SCHOOL

The school gates are closing,
The pupils trapped in.
They wait for the bell
Then lessons begin.

Heads down it's work time,
That's nothing new.
It's easy for others,
It isn't for you.

Playtime could kill you,
Don't get in the rush.
They pack through the doorways,
It's more like a crush.

Back to the classroom,
Clutching your pen.
You do the work right,
Or you do it again.

The bell rings for freedom,
Best hold your own.
They stampede through the exits,
It's time to go home.

Kristopher Welsh (11) Wardle High School

CRUELTY TO ANIMALS

Wherever you look,
Whoever you are,
there's always the animals,
Near and afar.

Cats in your living room,
Sheep on the farm
Rabbits in meadows,
Where everything's calm.

Parrots in cages,
Though they should be free,
Back in the jungle,
Up a green tree.

No-one owns an animal,
They belong to themselves,
It is due to us humans
That they walk in stealth.

Where are the dodos
Should they be there?
Already the rhinos,
Are living in fear.

Elephants and tigers,
And badgers are prey,
If they should see you
How long would they stay?

So stop polluting,
And help the world,
Stop killing the animals
Stop killing the world.

Kimberley Haigh (11) Wardle High School

THE WORLD'S PROBLEM

Dirty bottles, wrappers galore,
Pollution and litter on the world's floor,
Innocent animals die all the time,
Slaughter and hunt, a disgusting crime.

Forests are gone they are no more,
Wood choppers and carpenters galore,
We have enough to eat and drink,
But we are wasteful we do not think.

Smoke from the city,
Oh what a pity,
Children in Bosnia and Rwanda are
Hungry and thirsty.
If we act quick we can get there
Firstly.

So think about this and the things
I have said,
The world needs our help,
So don't let it down!

Ruth Harwood (11) Wardle High School

THE TIGER

With a silky coat of orange and black,
And big round innocent eyes,
The tiger prowls among the leaves
Under the shade of the moist rain forest.
Sharply he glances to the side
And pauses as he hears a rustle in the shrubs
He carries on cautiously, as silently as he can
He senses something nearby
He spies his prey, he freezes.
A group of birds are pecking the ground in
The clearing and he stalks slowly towards them.
He is now close enough to attack.
He crouches low and hesitates,
One, two, three he pounces,
He thrusts out his paws
Fluttering and screeching fill the air,
Rattling the branches,
The fortunate birds fly away
Not yet knowing that one of their friends
Is gone
Forever.

Lisa Sarasini (11) Wardle High School

THE BEGINNING TO THE END

When the sun and moon were one,
When the world had just begun
God left out one.

God made him a world of fire,
He made a world of pain.
Let us not forget that story, once again.

Then years later the stars fell
Like sheets of white from hell.
Now the devil comes to claim his land
From the desperate clutches of man's dark hands.

Christine Robinson (14) Westleigh High School

THERE'S NO TIME TO WAIT

I was happy until the news I saw,
Another death, another bomb,
And just one more pointless war.
Another child murderer and again a hit and run,
Teenagers killing just to have some fun.

When are the rest going to see?
Or is the dream of peace left up to you and me.
Us against this world of hate,
Someone must do something, we've got no time to wait.

Melanie Jackson (14) Westleigh High School

SAD ZOO ANIMALS

Once free, to roam the savannah,
Behaving in a proper manner,
Crowded together, monkeys behind bars,
To be laughed at by visitors, driving big cars,
Too many terrapins, they can't get on the beach,
The fish suffer from parasites like leech,
Dolphins and sealions forced to do unnatural tricks,
The mammal's fur is full of ticks.
The parrots must squabble to get a place on their perch,
And to fight for space, the wolves growl and lurch,
Zebra and antelope cannot even graze,
The killer whale, made to leap, is supposed to amaze,
The otters have no water, therefore cannot swim,
Their pool is full, up to the brim,
The pythons have grown, their terraria are too small,
Now their enclosures, they cannot house them all,
The eagles and vultures, they can't fly,
Their aviary is too small, that is why,
The seals have come, all the way from the shore,
They find life in this zoo, a terrible bore,
Where there are enough alligators, people add more,
Their standard of living, sinks lower and lower,
Hungry for food, the tigers are starving,
But people don't care whether or not they are thriving.
The nocturnal animals are constantly woken,
Because of a noisy human, with an entrance token,
The walrus pool is completely full, they are forced to the beach,
But when they are on there, they are within a human's reach,
The animals don't deserve this fate,
Just so someone can charge an entrance rate.

Allan Munro (14) Westleigh High School